THE
FRESH-WATER
FISHERMAN'S
BIBLE

Vlad Evanoff

THE FRESH-WATER FISHERMAN'S BIBLE

Illustrated by the author

DOUBLEDAY & COMPANY, INC.
GARDEN CITY, NEW YORK

ISBN: 0-385-03013-4

Library of Congress Catalog Card Number 63–16227
15   14

Contents

THE
FRESH-WATER
FISHERMAN'S
BIBLE

Chapter 1

BASIC FRESH-WATER FISHING OUTFITS

I started fresh-water fishing in the traditional country boy manner. When I needed a fishing "pole" I would look for the nearest long, straight tree sapling. Then I would take out my pocket knife and cut it down. After which I would get a length of string and attach a bent pin to the end for the hook. With this I caught sunfish and chubs in a small brook. Later I graduated to genuine fishhooks and long bamboo poles with which I caught panfish and trout. Still later I got a steel bait-casting rod and reel with which I could cast lures for bass and pickerel.

The bamboo cane pole is still a popular fishing tool with millions of fresh-water anglers. Such bamboo poles run anywhere from 8 to 20 feet in length. They come in one piece or in sections and can be broken down into three or four pieces for easy carrying and storing. You can buy such bamboo poles in most fishing tackle stores, sporting goods stores and country hardware stores.

If you want a stronger, longer-lasting pole you can get one of the telescopic glass poles which can be extended from a short 3 to 5 foot length to anywhere from 10 to 20 feet. They generally have from two to five sections which slide into each other.

These cane and glass poles are mostly used for still fishing with live baits especially for such panfish as sunfish, yellow perch, crappies, white bass, and bullheads. But they can also be used to work artificial lures or baits such as spoons, spinners, jigs, pork chunk, pork rind for the same panfish and occasional catches of bass, trout, pickerel, and other so-called game fish. Cane and glass poles, however, are limited to fishing short distances from shore, piers and boats.

Because of the many limitations of a cane or glass pole most fresh-water anglers turn to a more versatile outfit such as a rod and reel combination. These enable them to cast farther and offer more sport. Since World War II the spinning rods and reels have become very popular with fresh-water anglers. The spinning reels work on a "fixed-spool" principle and enable almost any angler to cast a light lure with only a little practice. There are no "backlashes" or "birdsnests" to plague an angler as in the days when only bait-casting reels were used.

There are now many different spinning outfits available for the fresh-water angler to handle almost any kind of fresh-water fishing. To simplify matters we can divide fresh-water spinning outfits into four groups: ultralight, light, medium, and heavy. The ultralight rod ranges from about 4½ to 6 feet in length and weighs from 1 to 3 ounces. With this light rod you can use one of the special ultralight open-faced reels such as the Alcedo Micron, Mignon 33, or the Garcia Mitchell 308. These ultralight reels weigh only from 5 to 8 ounces. The small reels are filled with monofilament line testing from ½ to 3 pounds. The whole outfit—rod, reel, and line—will weigh only about 7 to 10 ounces and is a pleasure to use.

The ultralight spinning outfit is best for small fish, small waters, and very light lures. It is

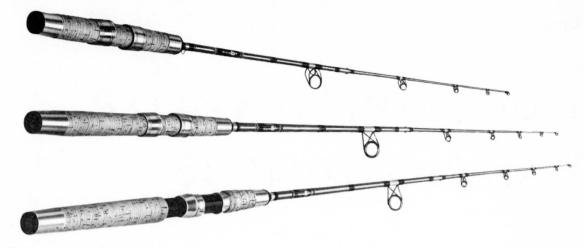

Garcia spinning rods are typical of the type used with open-faced spinning reels.

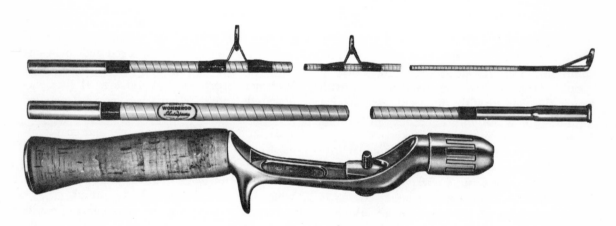

Shakespeare "Wonderod" is a spin-casting type of rod. Bait-casting rods are very similar, but usually have smaller guides.

ENLARGED HANDLE VIEW

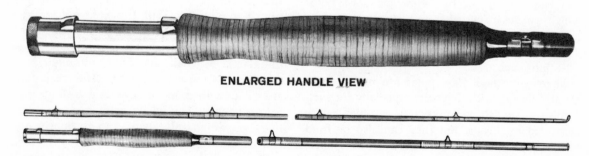

This is a Wright & McGill "Sweetheart" fly rod. They come in various lengths and weights for most fresh-water fly fishing.

often a deadly outfit when used for game fish such as trout and bass in low, clear, heavily fished waters. And you can't find a better outfit for sport and fun when seeking the smaller pan-fish. However, for the fresh-water angler who can afford only one spinning outfit the ultra-light is not the best one to get. It also requires quite a bit of practice and skill to use and is not for the casual or occasional fisherman.

The light fresh-water spinning rod and reel is more practical for fresh-water fishing in streams, rivers, and lakes. These rods will range from 6 to 7½ feet in length and weigh from 2 to 4½ ounces. Such a rod will cast lures weighing from ⅛ to ⅜ ounces. You can use this rod with most of the fresh-water spinning reels made, but the smaller, lighter models will balance the rod better. Monofilament lines testing from 3 to 6 pounds are usually used with the light spinning outfit, the 4-pound test being the most popular. The light spinning outfit is ideal for trout, small- or medium-sized bass, pickerel, and panfish.

The medium fresh-water spinning rod will also run from about 6 to 7½ feet in length. But it will be somewhat stiffer especially at the butt end and have a backbone to cast heavier lures and handle bigger fish. It will weigh from 4 to 6 ounces and can cast lures ranging from ¼ to ⅝ ounces. This includes most of the spinning lures made and many of the bait-casting lures which are too heavy to use with the lighter spinning rods. You can use almost any fresh-water spinning reel with this rod and it can be filled with lines testing from 4 to 8 pounds with the 6-pound the most popular. The medium-weight spinning rod is the nearest thing to an "all-around" rod for fresh-water fishing. It can be used for most of the fish found in fresh water such as bass, big trout, walleyes, pickerel, small pike, small catfish, and carp. You can use it to cast a lure or for bait fishing on the bottom with a light sinker. If you can afford only one rod for fresh-water fishing, the medium spinning rod is the one to get.

Heavy fresh-water spinning rods range from about 7 to 9 feet in length. They will weigh anywhere from 5 to 10 ounces and are used with the larger fresh-water spinning reels or small salt-water models. Lines testing anywhere

South Bend "Sup-matic" open-faced reel is similar to many types which come in different sizes for most fresh-water angling.

from 8 to 25 pounds are used with these rods and reels. The shorter rods in this class may be cast with one hand, but the longer ones have longer butts or handles for two-handed casting. Such rods will handle lures weighing anywhere from ½ to 2 ounces depending on the strength of the line and the power or action of the particular rod being used. Rods in the heavy class are used for big black bass, pike, muskellunge, steelhead, lake trout, and big carp and buffalo.

The heavy spinning rods are most suited for big fish, big waters, strong currents and fishing areas where there are many obstructions such as weeds, logs, sunken trees, and rocks. They can be used to cast heavy lures long distances and for fishing on the bottom with bait and sinkers.

In recent years the so-called "spin-casting" and "push-button" type reels have become very popular. These are similar to the open-faced spinning reels in that they also have stationary spools. But instead of having the spool exposed they have them covered. They are mounted above the rod like a bait-casting reel. In order to cast with them you simply push a button, then release it to send the lure out to the target. They are almost foolproof nowadays and very easy to use. They are also accurate and fast to use with less trouble from loose coils of line than the open-faced spinning reels.

The push-button type reels are now made in various sizes for use with lines testing anywhere from 4 to 20 pounds. The average reel of this type will hold from 80 to 150 yards of line which is enough for fresh-water fishing.

Garcia's "Abu-Matic" push-button or spin-casting reel can be used for a wide variety of fresh-water fishing.

The rods used with the push-button type reels are the spin-casting rods. These are similar to the bait-casting rods except that they have somewhat larger guides and are usually longer. Most rod manufacturers make the spin-casting rods in three or four different actions ranging from extra-light to light, medium, and heavy. The lighter rods of this type are used with lines testing 4 or 6 pounds and can cast lures of about ¼ ounce when required. The light and medium rods are used with 6- or 8-pound test lines and can cast lures ranging from ¼ ounce to ⅝ ounce in weight. The heavy spin-casting rods are used with the larger reels which hold lines testing from 10 to 20 pounds. These can cast lures weighing from ⅝ to 1½ ounces. Most spin-casting rods come in 6-, 6½-, or 7-foot lengths.

Most fly reels are either automatic or single-action. This Ocean City fly reel can be used either as an automatic or single action by simply adjusting the knob.

Pflueger "Supreme" bait-casting reel can be used with bait-casting type of rod for casting or trolling.

If you are buying your first casting rod for fresh-water fishing you can't go wrong by getting one of the spin-casting rods and push-button reels. For all-around use, the medium-weight rod is best. This can be used with an 8-pound test line for most fresh-water fishing. With such an outfit you can go out on a lake, river, or stream and in a short time learn how to cast a lure or sinker a good distance. With regular practice you will be able to cast accurately.

Then we have the bait-casting rods and reels which are used for many kinds of fresh-water fishing. These can be divided into three classes: light, medium, and heavy. The light bait-casting rod will run from 5½ to 6 feet long and has a limber action for casting light lures from ¼ to ½ ounce. It is used with the revolving spool level-wind bait-casting reel. For the light rod, the smaller, narrow spool bait-casting reel is best. This is filled with braided or monofilament lines testing from 6 to 10 pounds. The light bait-casting outfit is used for small- or medium-sized fish such as bass, big trout, pickerel, and large panfish.

The medium bait-casting rod runs from 4 to 6 feet in length and casts lures weighing from ½ to ¾ ounce. Since most bait-casting lures weigh around ⅝ ounce the medium bait-casting rod is perfect for handling such lures. The bait-casting reel used with this rod is filled with lines testing from 10 to 15 pounds. This rod makes a good all-around fresh-water tool for

Ocean City No. 940 is an all-purpose heavy-duty reel which can be used for casting, trolling, and still fishing for big fish in fresh water.

catching bass, walleyes, small pike, and muskies.

The heavy bait-casting rod ranges from 4 to 7 feet and is stiff and powerful for casting the heavier lures. Many of these rods will handle lures ranging from ¾ to 1½ ounces in weight. The bait-casting reel used with this rod can be filled with lines testing from 15 to 25 pounds. This rod is best for fishing for the larger game fish such as big black bass, pike, muskies, steelhead, Pacific salmon, and lake trout. It can also be used for bottom fishing with sinkers for such fish as catfish and carp. And it makes a good trolling rod for many fresh-water fish. The heavy bait-casting rod is best in waters with strong currents, or lakes or rivers filled with weeds, logs, rocks, or other obstructions.

Most modern bait-casting reels today are equipped with some kind of anti-backlash device which makes it easier to cast with than earlier models. However, it still requires more practice to cast far and accurately with a bait-casting reel than with one of the spinning or spin-casting reels. So when buying your first outfit it is better to get one of the spinning or spin-casting outfits. Later on, if you feel you need a bait-casting outfit, you can get one.

Many fresh-water anglers feel that for the most sport and thrills you can't beat a fly-fishing outfit. If you plan to do any trout fishing or Atlantic salmon fishing a fly rod is a must. For maximum sport from the smaller panfish go after them with a light fly rod.

Fly rods are made in various weights, lengths, and actions depending on where you are going to fish, the fish sought, lures used, and other conditions. Generally, the smaller the fish and the smaller the waters, the shorter and lighter the rod. For the bigger fish and big waters, the longer and heavier the rod. Also, for casting the heavier, bulkier lures long distances, the heavier and longer rods are more practical.

The lightest fly rods will range from 4½ feet up to 7½ feet. The shorter, lighter ones may weigh only an ounce while the longer ones in this class will run up to 4 ounces. They are used with the smallest fly reels to fish the smaller, heavier wooded streams where trout are not too big and casts are short. They are also fine for panfish and small bass.

Fly rods in the medium range will run from 7½ to 8½ feet in length and weigh from 4 to 5½ ounces. They are used with the smaller single-action or automatic fly reels. The rods in this class are used for general trout fishing in streams, rivers, and lakes. They are also good for bass and panfish and experts like to use them for Atlantic salmon and steelhead. Such a rod about 8 feet long is the nearest thing to an all-around rod for fly fishing with dry flies, wet flies, nymphs, streamers, and bass bugs.

Heavy fly rods range from 8½ to 9½ feet in length and may weigh anywhere from 5 to 7 ounces. Such rods are best for fishing big waters where big fish are often hooked and for making long casts. They are also the most efficient tools for casting the larger, bulkier lures such as streamers or bucktails and big bass bugs. This is the rod that is usually used for big trout on large rivers. It is also preferred for catching Atlantic salmon, steelhead, and big bass. If you plan to do a lot of bass-bug fishing for bass the heavy fly rod will do the job. The heavy fly rods are used with the largest single-action fly reels capable of holding the fly line and backing of braided nylon or Dacron. Anywhere from 100 to 200 yards of backing line is put on the reel to take care of long runs made by such fish as salmon and steelhead.

The fly line you use with the fly rods will depend on the type of fishing you will do. For casting dry flies a "double-tapered" floating fly line is best. For casting wet flies, nymphs, and streamers which are to be worked deep a "sinking" fly line is used. For casting bass bugs and for making long casts a "weight forward" or "bug taper" fly line is used. The size of the line used should match the fly rod you have. This information can best be obtained from the manufacturer who makes the rod. They usually list the correct size line to use in their catalogs or on the rod itself. Some tackle dealers who know fly tackle will also recommend the correct weight line to use with a particular fly rod.

Fresh-water anglers also use salt-water rods and reels at times for various kinds of fishing or in specific areas. Anglers seeking lake trout, for example, will often use salt-water boat or trolling rods and salt-water reels to handle the heavy wire lines and weights. If you plan to use wire lines for deep trolling make sure you get a reel with a metal spool.

Other anglers going after big carp, buffalo, catfish, or sturgeon may resort to salt-water spinning rods and reels or boat and surf rods and reels. They may also use the heavier salt-water lines testing from 20 to 40 pounds if they expect big fish in strong currents.

Before you buy any of the above tackle you should decide where you plan to fish and what kind of fish you expect to catch. Then you can make a wise choice as to the exact outfit you should get. Often you can obtain advice from an expert fishing friend as to the best outfit for the fishing in your area. Most fishing tackle dealers will also recommend the outfit which will serve your purpose if you will tell them where you plan to fish.

Fresh-water anglers also need various accessories such as boots or waders, vests or jackets, hat, fly or tackle boxes, landing net or gaff, fish stringer or creel, knife, pliers, oil, reel grease, sunglasses and insect repellent. And, of course, there are the various kinds of fishing lures, hooks, rigs, and baits which are required. These will be covered in each section dealing with a particular species of fish.

Chapter 2

WHAT MAKES A FISH POPULAR?

Fresh-water anglers in the United States and Canada are fortunate because they have a wide variety of species of fish to choose from in the streams, rivers, and lakes. There are several hundred species in this country with some states having as many as 150 species in their fresh waters.

This gives the fresh-water angler a wide choice in many areas. He can decide which fish he prefers and concentrate his efforts and time on catching that specific species. Or he can fish for one species and then when he gets tired of catching it he can shift his attentions to another kind of fish.

Fresh-water anglers tend to separate the various fishes into different groups. Some they call game fish and these are supposed to provide more sport on the end of the line than other kinds. Trout, salmon, and black bass are usually included in this group. Other fishes are called "panfish" and these are the smaller species such as sunfish, yellow perch, white bass, and crappies. Still others are called "rough" fishes and these include the carp, suckers, catfish, and eels.

But although some fish may be considered gamer and provide more sport than others, each fish mentioned above and others included in this book are admired and sought by fresh-water anglers. Fresh-water anglers go fishing for various reasons and not all of them agree on what qualities are most desirable in a fresh-water fish. Ask any group of fresh-water anglers which fish they prefer to catch and you'll wind up with a list of a dozen different species.

It all depends on what you are looking for in a fish. Do you want a fish that is powerful, fast, leaps high out of the water and puts up one of the most exciting fights in fresh water? Then you'll probably rate the Atlantic salmon and the Pacific steelhead as tops.

However, Atlantic salmon and steelhead are found only in certain waters and limited sections of this country and Canada. Also, fishing for Atlantic salmon can be expensive on many waters. So many other anglers settle for the rainbow trout which is another fast, flashy fighter often leaping out of the water.

Many anglers consider fly fishing as the most sporting method of all and any fish that can be caught on a fly, especially a dry fly, as the most desired species. These anglers rate such fish as the brook trout, brown trout, and rainbow trout superior to all others. Of the three trout above, many fly fishermen claim that the brown trout is the smartest and most difficult to catch. So the brown trout is more popular with the advanced or highly skilled anglers than either the rainbow or brook trout.

For the same reason, many fresh-water anglers consider the black bass, both the largemouth and smallmouth varieties as the smartest of the warm-water species. They claim that there is no fish more difficult to catch than a big, old bass which has been hooked a few times and is now wary and hard to fool. Such "smart" or "educated" fish offer a challenge to many anglers who would rather catch one fish that is hard to fool than a dozen other kinds which rush for the bait or hook.

To most kids any fish that bites on the particular day they are fishing is good enough. He's caught a couple of nice pickerel and some panfish in Belmont Lake, Pennsylvania. (PHOTO BY JOHNNY NICKLAS, PENNSYLVANIA FISH COMMISSION)

The largemouthed bass is highly popular because it is found in almost all the states and offers top sport, especially a big 4- or 5-pound fish like this taken on a fly rod. (TENNESSEE GAME AND FISH COMMISSION)

Another reason why the black bass is so popular is that it is now found in almost every part of the country. Black bass have been stocked in farm ponds, streams, rivers, lakes, reservoirs, and other bodies of water. From Canada south to Florida and west to California you'll find waters where black bass are present.

Another fish which has been stocked in many waters is the carp. Because the hardy carp can survive in waters too warm or too polluted for other fish, it is now found in many rivers and lakes throughout the country. Although many fresh-water anglers despise the carp and do not fish for it, there are other anglers who claim that carp are a lot of sport and fun on light tackle. Carp come big, too, with fish up to 20

and even 30 pounds caught in some waters. So they satisfy the desire of many anglers who want to catch something big.

Many other anglers who like to catch big fish will seek such species as pike, muskellunge, catfish, lake trout, and sturgeon. These anglers who seek these giants of the lakes and rivers feel that the smaller fish do not test their tackle or supply the thrills that the big fellows do. So they would rather catch one big fish than dozens of little ones.

Still other fish are popular because they make good eating and many anglers who like to eat fish will seek them out. For example, although the yellow perch isn't much as a fighter on the end of the line, it is tops in the frying pan. In

Panfish like this crappie are probably the most popular of all if we go by th' number of anglers seeking them. (LANG-LEY CORPORATION)

Trout are popular with many anglers especially in the spring. This is a scene at Montauk State Park, Missouri, on opening day. (FISH AND WILDLIFE SERVICE PHOTO BY REX GARY SCHMIDT)

fact, thousands of anglers would rather eat yellow perch than trout or bass and will spend much time fishing for them. Other fresh-water fish which make good eating include the eels, catfish and bullheads, walleye and most panfish.

Some fish are popular because they bite at night and can be caught during the hours of darkness. I know that some of my most memorable and thrilling fishing experiences as a boy occurred at night. We would go out to a nearby stream and fish for several hours for bullheads and eels. Other anglers in our southern states spend a lot of time fishing for catfish at night. Some of the largest game fish such as black bass, brown trout, and walleyes can be caught at night.

But the fresh-water fishes which are most popular are those which are most numerous and are easy to catch. In this class are the so-called "panfish," which attract more men, women, and kids than all the rest of the fish combined. They are usually caught with the least expensive and most simple tackle and bait. In many waters you can catch them from shore, docks, and piers. Or you can try for them from a small boat.

No doubt the most popular of the panfishes is the bluegill sunfish and the other members of the sunfish family. Then there are the crappies which are found in many of the larger rivers, lakes, and reservoirs. The white perch is a favorite in the eastern part of the country. The white bass has become very popular with panfishermen in our larger lakes, rivers, and reservoirs. Other panfish include the rock bass and yellow bass.

Nowadays, with more liberal fishing seasons and bag limits it is often possible to catch panfish all year round in our southern states. And they are often caught through the ice in the winter in our northern states. You can keep as many fish as you can use in many areas. There is no limit because panfish compete with game fish and other fish for living space and food. If there are too many panfish in a lake there will usually be fewer and smaller game fish. In fact, the panfish themselves may become stunted and fail to reach a good size. So the anglers who concentrate on catching panfish are often helping to produce better fish and fishing.

But no matter which fish you consider the most popular don't hesitate to try other kinds of fish and fishing. Too many fresh-water anglers get into a rut and spend most of their time fishing for one or two different kinds of fish. By doing this they are missing some fine sport and fun which can be obtained with other species. Each fish has its own characteristics and habits which makes it different from the others. Each has its peak season when it is most numerous and bites best. And each requires tackle, lures, baits, and methods and techniques which may differ from those used for other fish.

By going after as many different kinds of fresh-water fish as he can the angler acquires skills and experiences which make him a better "all-around" fisherman. And he learns to appreciate the qualities of each species and what it has to offer in the way of sport and fun.

These trout caught in a cold, clean, western mountain lake will make a mouth-watering meal. (JOHNSON MOTORS PHOTO BY RICHARD MATT)

Chapter 3

LARGEMOUTHED BASS

The largemouthed bass is one of the most widely sought of fresh-water game fish in the United States. It is especially popular with the expert and dedicated anglers who seek a challenge and a fish which is not too easily fooled. The largemouthed bass meets these requirements and is considered smart and unpredictable. They learn quickly from experience and avoid ordinary lures, baits, methods, and techniques. This is especially true when they get old and big and more wary.

Fortunately, however, largemouthed bass are also almost always hungry, curious, and pugnacious. If they don't hit a lure or bait because they are hungry, they may strike it because they are curious or angry. Time and again, anglers have seen bass who seemed indifferent to all the lures cast at them. But by continuous casting and reeling past their noses they finally succeeded in teasing the bass into grabbing the lure. They'll also guard their homes and nests against all intruders and chase and grab the largest lures.

Largemouthed black bass are often gluttons. They will fill their stomachs to capacity with large fish, frogs, mice, small birds, snakes, and young muskrats, and still hit a lure or bait. And if they can't find anything else they'll eat one of their own kind. Many a largemouthed bass has been found dead or dying with a smaller bass protruding from its mouth.

All this helps to make the largemouthed bass a worthy adversary on the end of the line. So when the black bass fishing season opens in our various states, millions of anglers head for their favorite pond, lake, or river to do battle with the beloved largemouthed bass.

At one time, the largemouthed bass had a limited range, being found mostly from southern Canada and Maine, through the Mississippi Valley to northern Mexico, the Gulf States and Florida and up along the East Coast. But extensive introductions have been made through the years and now you'll find largemouthed bass in almost every state. Together with the bluegill and the bullhead it has become one of the

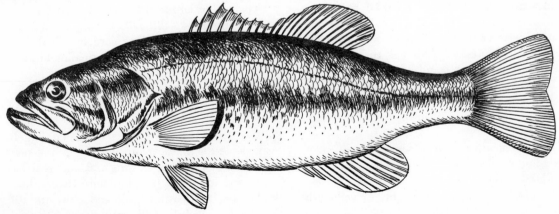

LARGEMOUTHED BASS

Largemouthed bass prefer lakes filled with stumps, weeds, lily pads, and similar cover. In such waters fish should be played carefully and it's handy to have another angler ready with the net. (EVINRUDE MOTORS)

favorite fishes to be stocked in farm ponds. It is more adaptable to various waters and water temperatures than the smallmouthed bass.

The largemouthed bass is also called the bigmouthed bass, green bass, green trout, lake bass, mossback, and linesides. Although there are several species of bass recognized by scientists, in this book we'll deal only with the largemouthed black bass and the smallmouthed black bass. The latter will be covered in the following chapter.

The largemouthed black bass varies in color depending on the waters where it is found. But generally it has a dark green or blackish back, lighter green on the sides and gray or yellowish white belly. There is a distinct black stripe run-

ning from the cheek to the tail. The eye is golden or amber colored. The maxillary or upper jaw of the largemouth extends past the eye, whereas in the smallmouthed bass it ends directly under the eye. The largemouthed bass is also less streamlined than the smallmouth and the larger ones tend to have pot bellies.

A few anglers fish for largemouthed bass with cane poles or glass poles but a casting rod of some type is much more sport and better in most waters. The black bass has been largely responsible for the development of the bait-casting reel and rod. The casting rod and reel has been used for black bass for more than a hundred years. Bait-casting rods and reels are still popular for black bass in many areas. They are

This big largemouth shows the dark line running from gill to tail which is found on most of these fish. It was caught in a reservoir near San Diego, California. (CALIFORNIA DEPARTMENT OF FISH AND GAME)

One of the most thrilling sights in fresh-water fishing is a largemouthed bass grabbing a surface plug or standing on its tail and shaking its head when hooked. (MICHIGAN TOURIST COUNCIL)

best when fishing in deep waters, for trolling, casting heavy lures, and in waters filled with obstructions. They are also best if the fish run very large as in many lakes and rivers in the South. Get a medium action bait-casting rod of from 5 to 6 feet long and a good level-winding bait-casting reel. Braided or monofilament lines testing from 10 to 18 pounds are used with these reels.

In spinning outfits try a medium spinning rod and a fresh-water spinning reel filled with 6-pound test for open waters and 8- or 10-pound test for snag-filled waters. A spin-casting or push-button type reel and rod can also be used for black bass with lines testing from 8 to 15 pounds.

Fly fishing for black bass calls for a fairly powerful rod about 8½ or 9 feet long. It is used with a single-action reel and a bug-taper or weight forward line to match the action of the rod. Although short level leaders have been used with such a fly outfit, a tapered leader about 9 feet long from 30-pound test at the butt section down to 8 or 6 pounds at the thin end is better.

When it comes to lures, for largemouthed bass there are thousands of plugs, spoons, spinners, jigs, plastic and rubber worms, eels and other imitations, pork chunk, pork rind, bass bugs and flies especially designed to catch largemouthed bass. A good basic assortment for the angler will include two or three different kinds of surface plugs like a popper, swimmer, gurgler, or wounded minnow, two or three shallow-running underwater plugs, two or three kinds of sinking or deep-running plugs, some weighted spinners, some spoons, plastic worms or eels and jigs. This will enable you to fish different depths, from top to bottom. There is no single lure or type of lure which will catch bass every day under all conditions. Most expert bass fishermen carry big tackle boxes filled with a wide variety of lures.

Largemouthed bass will also take almost any kind of natural bait—if it swims, crawls, or flies it is eaten by these bass. The time-honored worms are still good baits at times and you can use either night crawlers or the smaller garden worms. Frogs of smaller or medium sizes are also excellent baits. So are minnows of various kinds from 2½ to 3 inches long for small bass and up to 5 or 6 inches for big bass. In fact, in Florida they use small fish up to 8 or 10 inches for the lunker bass. Suckers, small bullheads, gizzard shad, small carp, goldfish, chubs, shiners, yellow perch, lamprey eels, and killifish can all be used where legal. Largemouthed bass have also been caught on hellgrammites, salamanders, leeches, crayfish, snakes, mice, crickets, grasshoppers, locusts, grubs, and nymphs.

The largemouthed bass spawns as early as February and March in the deep South and during May, June, and July in more northern climes. If the fishing season is open then you can have excellent action on the spawning beds. Largemouthed bass are very aggressive then and will strike at almost any lure which moves near them. The best fishing usually takes place in the spring and in the fall. But many bass are caught during the summer months although they may feed less frequently then and are harder to locate in the deeper waters.

When is the best time to go fishing for largemouthed bass? As a general rule during the bass season, which includes the summer months, you'll have your best luck early in the morning, in the evening, and at night for shallow water fishing. But when fishing in the middle of the day you can often catch them in deeper water. Early in the spring and in the late fall when the water is cold you'll often have your best action from 10 A.M. to 4 P.M. During the hot, summer months the dark, cloudy, rainy days are usually better than the bright, sunny days. And if you must fish during the summer months for bass, try to do as much fishing at night as you can. This is especially true on hard-fished lakes where there is also a lot of swimming, boating, and water-skiing activity.

Before fishing for largemouthed bass it's a good idea to establish the fact that the waters contain these bass. Usually you can obtain this information from other anglers, fishing tackle stores or other sources. Largemouthed bass are usually found in the warmer, sluggish rivers and weedy lakes with mud bottoms. However, some good fishing can also be experienced in some of the colder, clearer lakes with rock or gravel bottoms. But even there the largemouth tends to gather in areas where there are weed beds, lily pads, shallow coves, and backwaters.

In lakes, ponds and reservoirs largemouthed bass like to be under or near some kind of cover. They like the shady spots under lily pads, hyacinths, overhanging trees, or they lurk under driftwood, logs, brush, or around stumps, rocks, rocky points, piers, docks, boats, and rafts.

In rivers, they prefer the quieter portions, backwaters, eddies, coves and pools, especially those with weeds, sunken trees, logs or stumps.

These shallow-water spots near shore are usually the feeding places and large bass will defend them against all other bass and fish. However, when the water turns warm during the summer months bass will leave these shallow-water feeding places and head for deeper water nearby. These resting places are usually close to their feeding areas and may be over sunken weed beds or along drop-offs near shoals or reefs or bars. They usually move from the shallow areas to deep water and then back again to the feeding areas by the same route. So to enjoy good fishing you have to choose one of these three locations—shallow water, travel routes or the deep holes or resting places. The feeding or shallow spots are usually best early in the morning, in the evening, and at night. The deep-water resting places are best during the middle of the day. And the travel routes can be fished in-between these times.

The important point to remember in bass fishing, whether fishing in shallow water or deep water, is that bass are smart and wary. Especially the larger ones and when they are found in shallow water. A sloppy or noisy approach will scare them away or alert them. Expert anglers usually cut their motors when nearing a fishing spot and drift or row to the fishing area. Some even use two motors—a regular outboard to get to and from the fishing spot and a quiet electric motor for maneuvering the boat around the fishing areas. Canny bass anglers don't bang metal boxes, oars, or other objects against the boat. They try to do most of their fishing while sitting down. And in very clear or shallow water they make long casts in order to avoid being seen. At night they try not to use a flashlight unless absolutely necessary and then they don't shine directly on the water being fished.

Once you have located the bass your biggest problem is to find out which lure they want and how it should be presented and manipulated to bring a strike. If it is early in the morning or in the evening during the late spring and summer months a surface plug should be tried in shallow water. Such surface plugs as the poppers, swimmers, crippled minnows, darters, and gurglers which kick up a fuss on top are the ones to use. They are especially effective when the lake or river is calm. Most of them are supposed to imitate a crippled or injured minnow, so the action which duplicates the struggles of such a small fish is best.

First cast, then let the bait rest for a minute or two—then twitch it, let it rest, then jerk and twitch it again. Keep doing this all the way in.

Some of these plugs can be reeled in steadily but slowly, so that they roll, wobble, and crawl along the surface. And there are other times usually on the larger lakes and reservoirs where a torpedo-type surface plug can be reeled fast to bring a strike. This usually works best when the bass are schooled up and chasing minnows on the surface. Surface plugs are also very good to use at night.

Shallow-running underwater plugs can be used in shallow water near shore or in slightly deeper water up to a few feet. Some underwater plugs run only a few inches to a couple of feet under the surface while others may go down somewhat deeper. Usually slow reeling will keep them closer to the surface, while faster reeling will make them dive deeper. Most of these plugs have a built-in action such as a wriggle, dart, or wobble, but you can also give them added action by varying the speed of the retrieve and occasional jerks of the rod tip. Shallow-running underwater plugs can be used throughout the day and also at night. They are often better than surface plugs when the water is choppy or rough or discolored.

Deep-running and sinking plugs are used in deeper water usually from 8 to 30 feet deep. Some of these plugs have long lips and dive to depths of about 20 feet. Others of the sinking

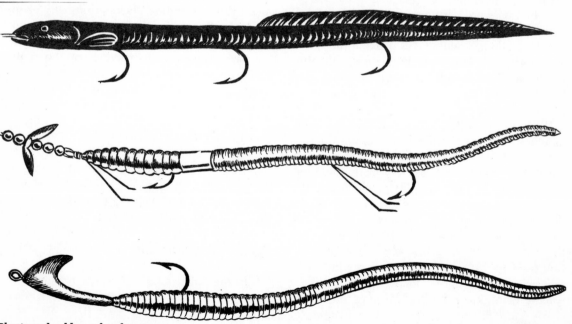

Plastic and rubber eel and worms

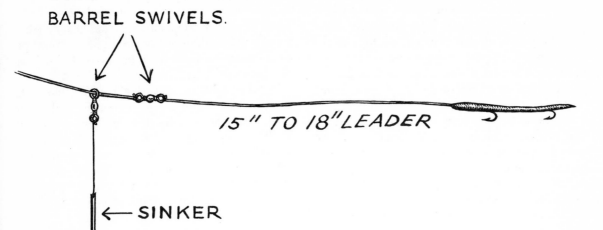

BARREL SWIVELS.

15" TO 18" LEADER

←— SINKER

Rig for fishing plastic worm

type go down slowly to even deeper bottoms but must be reeled very slowly to stay there. They are most effective during the middle of the day when bass are lying in the sunken weed beds, off rocky points, drop-offs, and in holes.

In recent years anglers have accounted for some big bass with various kinds of rubber and plastic worms and eels. Some are also made from pork rind. They are long and slender, come in various colors with the black, brown, white, red, and yellow the most effective. Some have spots and others are even smeared with some kind of oil or scent to attract fish. Some of these worms and eels have only one hook, while others have two or three. Some have extra weight, while others have lead heads or jig heads up front to make them sink faster and make it easier to bounce bottom. And still others have small spinners or gold bands for added attraction.

The unweighted worms or eels can also be fished with a rig and a light sinker as shown in the illustration. Or you can add a small clincher to the leader about two feet above the lure to get it down into the depths. Usually these plastic worms and eels are used in deep water during the middle of the day and are crawled or bounced along the bottom as slowly as possible with pauses and short jerks of the rod tip to supply action to the lure.

When fishing rocky points or shores with sloping banks and rocky ledges you can anchor in deeper water, cast toward shore and let the plastic and rubber worms bounce from rock to rock on the way down. The weighted ones with jig heads are best for this kind of fishing.

The unweighted plastic and rubber lures can be worked near the surface by reeling and providing rod action. And you can cast them near shore around weeds, lily pads, stumps, rock or gravel bars, and work them steadily but slowly allowing them first to sink then raise the rod and let them come up, then sink again and raise again.

When using two or three hooks with the plastic worms or eels you can strike as soon as you feel the hit. With a single hook in the lure you should give the bass time to grab the worm or eel, hold on to it and then swallow it, before you strike back.

Another good deep-water lure for largemouthed bass is the lead head jig which was formerly mostly a salt-water lure. These also come in various weights, sizes, and colors with black, yellow, brown, and white the most popular. They are often used with a strip of pork rind on the hook.

Jigs are cast out in deep water until they hit bottom, then they are bounced slowly and raised and lowered along the weed beds, rocky ledges, and in holes where bass are lying.

Spoons are old-time large-mouth lures but they are still effective in many waters and on many occasions. Around the lily pads you can use a silver, gold, or copper spoon with a weedless hook and a strip of pork rind. Cast right into the pads and pull it along the tops of the plants until the spoon comes to an open pocket of water. Then let it sink a few inches and reel and jerk it until it comes up to the pads again. Other times you can use the spoons in open waters especially when you see bass schooled up and chasing minnows or other small fish. And on still other occasions you can cast near shore allowing the spoon to sink a few inches then retrieve it in a darting, stop-and-go retrieve with erratic action with the rod tip.

Pork chunks and frogs are also good lures to use around lily pads, hyacinths, and other weeds and vegetation. They should be used with a weedless hook and are cast into the pads and retrieved so that they slither and hop along the tops of the pads and through the open pockets. Hold your rod tip high when you do this.

Bass bugs are great lures to use with the fly rod when the largemouths are in the shallows near shore. The various cork, plastic, and deer hair poppers, frogs, bugs and minnows are all good at different times. They are used around weed beds, lily pads, stumps, logs, and rocks near shore. Most of the bugs should be worked very, very slowly with long rests, pauses, short jerks and twitches to imitate a bug, moth, dragonfly, or other insect or a small frog. The minnow-type bugs can be retrieved more steadily and faster to simulate a frantic minnow trying to escape. Streamers and bucktails can also be used this way.

When casting doesn't produce or you want to locate bass in a strange lake, trolling can be tried. Here, you can use spoons, underwater plugs, spinners and worms, or minnows and troll them at various depths until you find the fish.

In the morning and evening you can troll close to shore along the edges of lily pads, over weed beds, around rocky points and sand or rock bars. During the middle of the day trolling should be done in deeper water with lures that travel near the bottom or even bump it.

A lot of bass are still caught on natural baits such as live frogs, worms, minnows, and other creatures. This can be done without a float in shallow water and in open waters. But in deeper water a bobber or float is better to keep the bait off the bottom and away from weeds and to indicate a bite. In any kind of live bait fishing for bass let them swallow the bait before trying to set the hook.

Largemouthed bass put up an exciting fight, often standing on their tails and shaking their heads violently to throw the lure. They should be played carefully until they give up before an attempt is made to boat them. This can be done with a net leading the bass head-first into it. Some anglers also grab the bass by the lower lip but this can be dangerous if plugs are used.

In most of our northern lakes, largemouthed bass will run from 1 to 4 pounds in weight. A 5- or 6-pound largemouthed is a big one in these waters. Farther south fish grow much bigger and the lunkers are more numerous. Here a bass must reach 8 or 10 pounds before it is considered large. The world record on rod and reel is a 22-pound, 4-ounce largemouthed bass taken by George Perry in Montgomery Lake, Georgia, on June 2, 1932.

Largemouthed bass are found in so many waters all over the country that it would require a book to list them all. In fact, there is a book which lists the top bass waters state by state. It is *The Bass Fisherman's Bible*, written by Erwin A. Bauer and published by Doubleday & Company.

Chapter 4

SMALLMOUTHED BASS

Most anglers like to fish for both the largemouthed bass and the smallmouthed bass, but those who have caught both species agree that, when it comes to fighting, the smallmouth has a slight edge. This is especially true when comparing the smallmouth of the fast, cold rivers with the largemouth of the warm, muddy lakes. But even when both are found in the same waters, the smallmouthed has that extra dash, speed, and stamina which makes him the superior battler.

Unfortunately, not every angler gets the opportunity to fish for smallmouthed bass. These fish cannot stand very warm waters nor do they thrive as well in small, still waters as the largemouth. So they cannot live in as many areas and different climates as the largemouth. Smallmouthed bass like the cooler, cleaner, swifter rivers and the deep, cool, rocky lakes. Such waters are not as numerous as the warm, muddy, weedy lakes and ponds which the largemouth

prefers. So, while the smallmouth has been introduced into most of our states there are vast areas in the South and West where smallmouthed bass are scarce or absent.

Originally the smallmouth was found from southern Canada south to Alabama and Georgia. But it has been introduced throughout New England, along most of the East Coast and from California to British Columbia.

The smallmouthed bass has also been called the black perch, brown bass, tiger bass, swago bass, gold bass, redeye, bronze bass, and bronzeback. The smallmouth will vary in color from a pale yellow to a dark brown, depending on where it lives. Usually it is a dull olive-gold with a luster of bronze. The belly varies from a creamy white to a gray. The sides will usually have dark bars, bands, and patches. The eye of a smallmouth is bright red. The maxillary or upper jaw reaches only to the middle of the eye and not beyond as in the largemouthed bass.

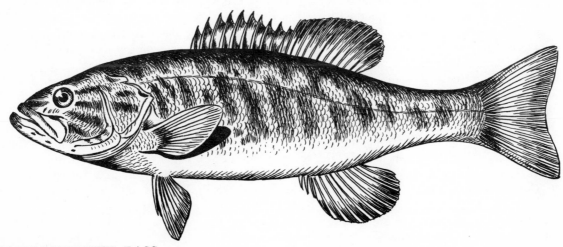

SMALLMOUTHED BASS

Smallmouthed bass are great fighters on light tackle like this spinning outfit. (LANGLEY CORPORATION)

You can use the same kind of tackle for small-mouthed bass as for the largemouthed bass. The same bait-casting, spinning, spin-casting, and fly tackle covered in the previous chapter can be used also for smallmouthed bass fishing.

The same is true of the lures such as surface and underwater plugs, spoons, spinners, plastic and rubber worms and eels, jigs, bass bugs, and flies. However, as a general rule you'll find that the smaller and lighter lures are better for smallmouthed bass than the larger, heavier lures often used for largemouthed bass.

The smallmouthed bass will also take many of the natural baits which appeal to the large-mouthed bass. The favorites are usually worms, minnows, hellgrammites, crayfish, lamprey eels, frogs, crickets, and grasshoppers.

The seasons for smallmouthed bass will, of course, depend on when the laws permit fishing for these popular fish. They are often protected when on the spawning beds especially in northern waters. Smallmouthed bass may be caught in the southern areas where they are found as early as March or April, but farther north the fishing usually doesn't start until May or June. June is a good month in many areas and is especially productive in Maine. Fishing in Canada and also in many of our northern states may be fair to good during July and August. September and October are usually top months for smallmouthed bass fishing in many waters.

In the spring and again in the fall, small-mouthed bass can be found in the shallows most of the day. Later on, during the hot summer

A fine catch of good-sized smallmouthed bass taken from Lake Wallenpaupack, Pennsylvania. (PHOTO BY JOHNNY NICKLAS, PENNSYLVANIA FISH COMMISSION)

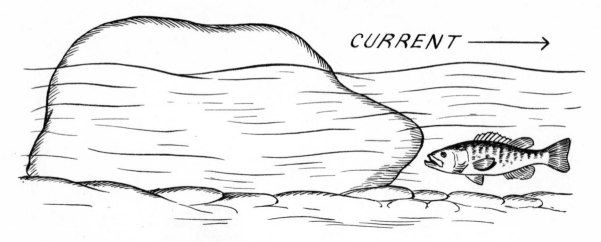

CURRENT ⟶

Smallmouthed bass often lie below a boulder.

months, the shallows should be fished early in the morning, late in the evening, and at night. At this time they will often come into shallow water to feed on minnows, crayfish, and various bugs and flies. In the summer you can sometimes catch them during the daytime by fishing the deep holes and pools. When the water is low and clear and warm in a river wait for a shower or rain which raises the level of the water, lowers the temperature and makes it slightly brown. Then the bass may go on a feeding spree and you'll have fast action.

In rivers look for smallmouthed bass in the rocky stretches especially where there is fairly deep water with plenty of big rocks and boulders scattered throughout. They'll be found lying behind and beneath these boulders, ledges, and in the pockets in-between the boulders. When actually feeding they will often come into the rapids, riffles, and fast runs and shallow tails and heads of pools. Other times, they will be lurking in the deeper pools and eddies and backwaters. In the bend or curve of a river they'll often be lying on the deeper side under rock ledges, behind rocky outcroppings and under the banks.

In lakes, they prefer the rocky shores, bottoms of rock, sand or gravel, and the offshore bars and reefs. Sunken weed beds and rocky bottoms in 8 to 20 feet of water are also good since minnows and crayfish often abound there. But don't pass up the spots in the lake usually associated with largemouthed bass. Such as stumps, logs,

brushpiles, sunken trees, coves, and weedy shores. In the summer, smallmouthed bass will be in the deeper holes and around the cooler spring holes. Sharp drop-offs near reefs and shoals will often hold small schools of fish. In lakes during hot weather fish the inlets of streams or rivers entering into the lake or even the river or stream itself.

When fishing the narrower or small streams and rivers for smallmouthed bass, they should be approached carefully and quietly. These waters are often shallow, clear, and narrow—smallmouthed bass are very spooky here and will take off for deeper water or hide under a rock at the slightest disturbance. Try to avoid wading if possible and make your casts from shore. If you do have to wade do it slowly without creating too much of a disturbance and watch where your shadow falls.

Smallmouthed bass will often take surface plugs worked like a crippled minnow or frog near shore in shallow water. In rivers you can cast among boulders and rocks and work the plug through the pockets where bass may be lying.

Spoons and weighted spinners also account for many smallmouthed bass especially in rivers. Here you can cast upstream and across and let the lure sink a few inches. Raise the rod and reel in fast. Next stop, lower the rod and let the spoon sink once more—then raise the rod and speed up your reeling. This gives the spoon a tumbling crazy action which often brings strikes.

A weighted spinner can be worked in much the same way, but can also be reeled straight and jerked at regular intervals with the rod tip. If high retrieves fail to bring a strike let the spoon or spinner sink deeper. Try different levels right down to the bottom.

Small underwater plugs are often effective in lakes and rivers. In shallow water those that float and dive and wriggle a few inches below the surface or a bit deeper are best. These usually have a built-in action, but sometimes rod action and a change of speed of the retrieve is needed to bring strikes. For deeper waters, the deep-diving or sinking plugs are better. These should usually be worked as close to the bottom as possible. In fact, you can even let the diving plugs dig into the bottom and stir up some mud and sand. Plugs of this type that imitate crayfish are especially effective.

Other good bottom-bouncing lures when smallmouths are deep are the weighted lead jigs, the plastic worms and eels, and bucktails and spinners. All of these should be worked right on the bottom in the deep holes, sunken weed beds and drop-offs where smallmouths might be lying.

Fly rod anglers will find the various bass bugs, streamers, bucktails, wet flies, and at times dry flies, effective for smallmouthed bass. These usually work best near shore and in rivers in the early morning, late afternoon, and evening when flies are hatching and bugs are numerous. But bass bugs of the minnow type and streamers and bucktails are also effective when smallmouths are feeding on minnows in the shallows or tails of pools. These should be cast and retrieved by stripping in line in spurts and an erratic manner to simulate a frightened or frantic minnow.

Trolling is often deadly when smallmouthed bass are in water from 6 to 20 feet deep. This can be done with an outboard motorboat at slow, medium, and fairly fast speeds with lines from 30 to 100 feet out. The lures should travel down close to the bottom. It will require experimentation to find out which lures are best, the right speed to use for them and how much line to let out. Such lures as underwater plugs, spoons, spinners, and steamers can be used in trolling.

Smallmouthed bass are not always easy to catch with artificial lures and there are times when natural baits are much more effective. Then you can drift a worm or hellgrammite in a river so that it tumbles with the current and moves into holes, pockets, or alongside crevices or undercut banks where smallmouths are lying.

Good catches with live baits can often be made in rivers or streams which are muddy if you know exactly where the bass are lying. Then you can drift the worm or hellgrammite or minnow right in front of the fish. They can't see too far in such roiled waters so you have to hit them right on the nose.

Still fishing in the deeper pools, eddies, holes, drop-offs, and sunken weed beds with live bait can be done from an anchored boat or from shore. From a boat you can often fish without a sinker and merely lower the bait to the bottom. From shore or even from a boat when fishing in fast currents a small sinker can be tied on the end of the line and a long leader and hook above it to get the bait out and keep it down.

Besides worms and hellgrammites you can use frogs and crayfish for smallmouthed bass. Crayfish are best if used when they are in the soft-shelled stage and here you'll often have to tie them on the hook carefully to keep them from falling off. Frogs are hooked through the lips or a leg and are effective when used near shore or in shallow water or quiet pools in rivers and streams. Crayfish should be used in rocky areas and in deep water holes close to the bottom, or on the bottom where they are usually found.

Other effective smallmouthed bass baits at times are live grasshoppers or crickets. A small, light wire hook about size No. 5 is best for these small insects. They are hooked lightly and cast out on top of the water where they can kick around. If that fails, let them sink to various depths and even down to the bottom.

When using most natural baits give the bass plenty of time to swallow them before setting the hook. This is especially true with big baits such as frogs, hard crayfish or minnows which take time to engulf and swallow.

A smallmouthed bass on the end of a line in a fast river will put up a fight which will remind you of a trout. He will often make a long, fast run, or leap out of the water or he'll sound and bore for some rocks or snags. In the deeper waters of lakes he may do most of his fighting

You'll often find smallmouthed bass in rivers with deep, fast currents in our northern states and Canada. The spot where rapids or falls spill into a deep pool is especially productive. (EVINRUDE MOTORS)

below the surface, but even here he'll usually show more speed, flash, and endurance than the largemouthed bass.

Most smallmouthed bass in rivers will run from one-half of a pound to about 3 pounds in weight. Any fish going 4 or 5 pounds is a big one in northern waters whether caught in a river or a lake. In southern states such as Kentucky and Tennessee they may reach large weights because of the longer feeding and growing seasons and abundance of food in the larger reservoirs. That's where the 11-pound 15-ounce rod and reel record smallmouthed bass was taken in Dale Hollow Reservoir on the Tennessee-Kentucky border by D. H. Hayes in 1955.

However, the southern lakes and reservoirs are usually better suited for largemouthed bass than the smallmouthed bass. If you want good smallmouthed bass fishing you're better off if you fish such rivers as the Delaware, Susquehanna, St. Lawrence or in our northern states such as Maine, Vermont, New Hampshire, New York, Pennsylvania, Ohio, Michigan, Wisconsin, and Minnesota. And Canada offers some great smallmouthed bass fishing, especially in Ontario and to a limited extent in New Brunswick and Quebec.

Chapter 5

ATLANTIC SALMON

Ask any expert fresh-water angler which fish he considers the greatest game fish in fresh water and chances are he'll say the Atlantic salmon. This big fish is highly revered and esteemed by anglers not only in America but also in Europe.

Through the centuries the Atlantic salmon has been prized not only for sport but also for food. In England, Scotland, and in this country, Atlantic salmon were once so plentiful that they were served every week at meals for servants and workers. Some of them even complained if they had to eat salmon more than twice a week.

That, of course, was in the good old colonial days when Atlantic salmon swarmed up the coastal rivers as far south as the Connecticut River. But during the last century Atlantic salmon have been depleted by commercial fish-ing, heavy sport fishing, pollution, dams, and changing conditions of our coastal rivers.

Nowadays, Atlantic salmon are found in Maine, Canada, the British Isles, Norway, Sweden, Finland, Iceland, France, and Spain.

As almost everyone knows, Atlantic salmon ascend fresh-water rivers to spawn after spending from one to six years in the ocean. Those that return to the stream after one year are called grilse and range from 3 to 6 pounds in weight. The fish which spend two or three years in the sea are much larger when they return to spawn, sometimes reaching 20 to 30 pounds in weight. Salmon which spend longer periods living in the ocean reach the heaviest weights.

An Atlantic salmon just entering the fresh waters of a river is a handsome fish. It has a dark

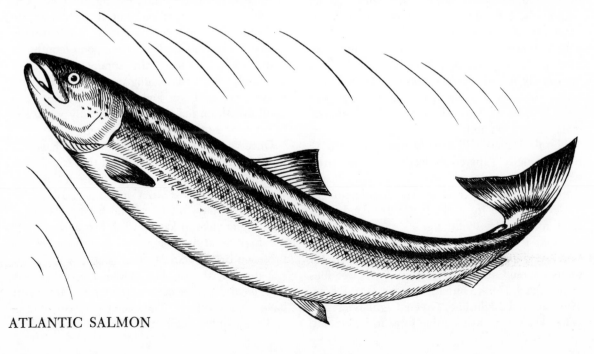

ATLANTIC SALMON

steel-blue back, silvery sides, and white belly. Small black spots may cover the back and sides. After spending some time in fresh water the salmon loses its silvery coat which turns dull and reddish or gray. The spots grow larger toward spawning time. After spawning they become even more drab and also lose weight. Then they are called "black" salmon or kelts. These spent fish are often caught on their way back to the ocean, but most expert salmon anglers consider them inferior in fighting ability and endurance to the "bright" salmon which are fresh-run from the sea.

Atlantic salmon can only be caught in this country and Canada on fly fishing tackle. At one time, long, double-handed salmon fly rods from 12 to 16 feet long and weighing up to 26 ounces were used. A few such rods are still being used in Europe for big fish and heavy waters. But the trend nowadays is toward lighter tackle and fly rods from 7½ to 9½ feet are preferred. The longer, heavier rods are best for big waters and big fish especially early in the spring In the smaller rivers and for small fish and for dry fly fishing, the shorter, lighter rods are used.

The single-action reel used for salmon fishing should be larger than most trout reels. It should hold your fly line together with at least 150 to 200 yards of backing line. The backing line can be of braided nylon or Dacron testing around 15 pounds. A floating, weight forward fly line is good for all-around salmon fishing and allows you to make long casts. But many salmon anglers prefer tapered or double-tapered fly lines for dry fly fishing Still others like sinking lines rather than the floating types for use with wet flies. Whichever line you use, will, of course, match your rod and bring out its action.

The fly leaders will usually run from 9 to 12 feet in length. Tapered fly leaders are preferred with the heavier tapers used for big fish, heavy waters, and wet fly fishing. The lighter, longer leaders are used for clear, low-water conditions, small fish and dry fly fishing.

When it comes to flies for salmon the old, standby, gaudy, wet patterns specially tied for salmon should always be carried. Such wet flies as the Black Dose, Durham Ranger, Cosseboom, Thunder and Lightning, Green Highlander, Silver Gray, Silver Doctor, Blue Charm, Jock Scott,

Silver Wilkinson, Dusty Miller, March Brown, Lady Amherst, and Mar Lodge have taken many fish in the past and continue to do so. Wet flies in the larger sizes from 5/0 down to No. 2 are used in the early spring when the water is high and roily. Later on flies in sizes No. 4, 6, 8, or 10 can be used with the smallest sizes used when the river is low and clear.

Dry flies for salmon include such patterns as the Wilkinson, the Cahills, Pink Lady, White Wulff, Grey Wulff, Whiskers, Irresistible, Hendrickson, Mackintosh, and the various Bi-visibles and Spiders. Dry flies in sizes No. 6, 8, and 10 are usually used but at times you may want a larger fly in sizes No. 2 or 4 to raise certain fish.

The key to success in Atlantic salmon is to time your fishing trip to coincide with the runs of the fish upstream. It is important to be at the river when the fish are entering fresh water. The exact day when this occurs varies from river to river and from year to year. It depends on many factors such as the weather, water temperature, water level, and time of year. Salmon like to move into the rivers when they are high from recent rains. Then they move fast from pool to pool often covering many miles in a short time. When the river is low the salmon may not enter and wait at the estuaries. Or they may move up to a deep pool or hole and wait there for the river to rise. Good salmon fishing can be experienced as early as April on some rivers and as late as October on others. The spring run is usually the best with May and June two good months on many waters. During the summer months of July and August the fishing may be fair to good if the river isn't too low. September may be a good month on many rivers especially when the fall rains raise the level of the water.

Once you are on the salmon river you have another vital problem to solve. And that is to locate the spots where the salmon are lying in the river. Casting blindly as is often done when fishing for trout rarely pays off in salmon fishing. Most expert anglers like to locate a fish first and actually see him or at least have an indication of his presence before they start casting.

Naturally, the natives of the area or anglers who have fished a certain river for many years have an advantage. They have seen many fish or have caught them in certain spots and know

Hugh Grey, editor of Field & Stream *magazine, holds a young salmon or "grilse." These smaller salmon usually are faster and livelier than the bigger ones.* (CANADIAN GOVERNMENT TRAVEL BUREAU)

where to look for them. That is why an angler fishing a certain river for the first time will get much quicker results if he hires a guide. The guides are familiar with the river, know the habits of the salmon and know where they are lying under various water conditions. On certain rivers in Canada you must hire a guide if you fish from a boat. But even when fishing from shore a guide can be a big help.

If you are on your own, you can try to locate a fish in shallow water in depths anywhere from 3 to 8 feet deep. It is usually best to concentrate on the pools, especially the swift, shallow pools rather than the deep, quiet ones. Look for rocks or boulders around which the current flows past. The eddies behind such rocks will often hold salmon. Or they may be lying alongside a rock or boulder which splits the fast current. Look for them around gravel bars, the tails of pools and along the deep-cut banks and ledges. If a river forms a lake, look for salmon at the inlets and outlets.

At times you can also see them leaping or rolling on the surface. Leaping salmon are less likely to strike your fly than one which just barely shows its back or fins above the water.

Salmon can be caught throughout the day early in the season when the waters are high and cold. Later on during the hot summer months, when the water is low and clear, better results are obtained early in the morning and in the evening.

The method of presentation of the wet fly differs from that usually used in trout fishing. Instead of casting upstream for salmon the cast is generally made across and downstream and the fly is allowed to swing in an arc. If you see the salmon or know which way he is facing try to present the fly broadside to him. The fly can also be retrieved in short jerks against the current or can be picked up at the end of the drift and a new cast made.

When fishing water where the exact position of the fish is uncertain or where several fish may be lying, you can start with short casts and then lengthen them to cover all the water. Then you can move to a new position downstream and cast in an arc to cover new water.

As a general rule it is best to have the wet fly travel just below the surface or not too deep. However, there are times in deeper pools or runs

when it pays to let the fly sink and drift closer to the bottom. The main idea is to let the fly drift naturally with little or no drag. You may have to raise or lower your rod tip to control the slackness or tightness of the line on the water. You may also have to mend your line by rolling it upstream so that it makes a curve on the upstream side to enable the fly to drift without drag or unnatural fast swing.

When fishing wet flies from a boat with a guide you will, of course, follow his instructions on what fly to use, where to cast and how to work the fly. Casts from a boat are usually made on both sides with the line being lengthened to cover most of the water. Then the boat may be moved downstream by the guide to a new spot where the procedure is repeated.

During the summer months when the water is low and warm, salmon will often rise to a dry fly more readily than a wet one. Here too, instead of casting upstream, you try to cast across or downstream well above the fish so that the fly drifts over him. Salmon aren't as frightened as trout at seeing an angler nearby. So you don't have to sneak up on them or use too long a line. However, it is wise not to get too close—or make any unnecessary movements. The dry fly should float without drag most of the time. But there are times when you can deliberately drag a fly with a short twitch or jerk to try to induce a strike.

The thing to remember is that Atlantic salmon feed little if at all when in fresh water. So they aren't too interested in your offering. With luck you may get a strike early after a few casts—or you may have to make a hundred casts before a salmon suddenly decides to take it. Of course, in rivers where fish are plentiful you don't have to make too many casts over the same fish. You can make a couple of dozen casts with different flies and then move down to the next fish or hot spot. But in rivers where fish are scarce or fishing spots few, you may have to spend a lot of time casting to one or two fish.

Salmon are slower and more deliberate about taking a fly than a trout. So don't strike too fast when you see the fish rise or flash. Wait a second or two to allow the fish to clamp his jaws on the fly before you set the hook. Salmon also have a habit of striking short or changing their minds at the last minute. Such fish are often

Any day you can catch three beautiful Atlantic salmon like these is a red-letter day. (CANADIAN GOVERNMENT TRAVEL BUREAU)

hooked on succeeding casts if you continue to present the fly to them.

Once hooked, a salmon may make a long, fast run or leap high out of the water or walk on its tail. Its acrobatics and long, powerful runs make him one of the top fighters to be found in fresh water. Fight a salmon directly from the reel instead of holding the line as when fighting a small trout. And keep a light drag on the reel in the beginning to permit the fish to take line freely. Try to stay abreast or below the fish at all times. If the fish takes off downstream you have to follow it until you come abreast of it again. Many big fish are lost in fast shallow rapids when they tear downstream and take all the line or break off.

If there's a sand or gravel beach or bar, you can often beach the fish in shallow water and then pick it up under the gills. Nets are used by many guides when fishing from a boat. A tailer which snares the fish around the tail by means of a wire noose is preferred by many salmon anglers. Gaffs have also been used but they may injure a fish which later escapes. Expert anglers sometimes grab a salmon around the narrow part of the tail with their hands.

Most of the salmon you'll catch will range in weight from 3 to 20 pounds. Big salmon from 20 to 50 pounds are not too plentiful in most rivers. The largest ones are usually caught in Europe, especially in Norway. The rod and reel record is a 79-pound 2-ounce fish caught in 1928 by Henrik Henrikson in Norway. One of the largest ever recorded weighed 103 pounds and was killed by Scottish poachers at the mouth of the Devon River in 1902.

Atlantic salmon make fine eating but most anglers don't fish for them because of their food value. Salmon are sought and caught because most fresh-water anglers find them an unpredictable and difficult fish to hook or land. They offer a challenge to anglers not provided by most other fresh-water fish.

Fortunately in recent years what with increased leisure time, better roads and cars, jet plane travel and more and more public waters on the different salmon rivers it is possible for the average angler to enjoy Atlantic salmon fishing.

In the United States the Atlantic salmon is found only in the State of Maine. Here such rivers as the Penobscot, Aroostook, Machias, Dennys, Narraguagus, Pleasant, Sheepscot, Tunk Stream, and Little Falls can be fished. The total take of salmon on all the Maine rivers is not too big, usually numbering several hundred fish each season. But not too many out-of-state anglers fish these waters and most of the salmon are caught by local fishermen. There is plenty of room and enough fish in Maine waters to accommodate many more anglers.

In Canada, New Brunswick offers some of the best salmon fishing despite its nearness to the United States. There, the famed Miramichi river system alone has produced up to 18,000 salmon on rod and reel in one year. Rivers such as the Cains, Dungarvon, Renous, Tobique, Upsalquitch, Tabusintoc, Restigouche, Sevogle, Bar-

tholomew, and St. John's are among the best known. In New Brunswick most of the waters are private or leased, but there are stretches open to the public.

Nova Scotia has over forty salmon rivers and all of them open to the public at the cost of a fishing license. Such rivers as the Medway, Tangier, Gold, Margaree, Tusket, Moser's, and St. Mary's are best known and the most productive.

In Quebec until recently all waters were private or leased, but now there are public waters on such rivers as the Matane, Port Daniel, and Little Cascapedia.

In Newfoundland, all the rivers are open to the public and the best ones are the Humber, Grand Codroy, Little Codroy, Serpentine, Portland Creek, and Harry's River. Most of the salmon caught in Newfoundland are the smaller grilse which average about five pounds. But what they lack in size they make up in numbers and spirit.

In Labrador, all the rivers are also open to the public and the top waters here are the Forteau, Pinware, Eagle, and Adlatok. Because of the distance and difficulty in reaching the rivers and the lack of accommodations, Labrador rivers haven't been fished too heavily. But more and more anglers are visiting these virgin waters as roads are being built and places to stay are established.

Chapter 6

LANDLOCKED SALMON

Thousands of anglers in our New England states and Canada eagerly await the cry "the ice is out" on their favorite lake containing landlocked salmon. Then regardless of the weather which can be raw in April in northern climes, they converge on the lake and spend hours trolling or casting from small open boats.

The fish they are seeking—the landlocked salmon—is almost identical to the great Atlantic salmon which runs up rivers to spawn from the sea. The main difference is that the landlocked salmon like its name implies is trapped in fresh water and doesn't migrate to the sea. Landlocked salmon are also smaller than the Atlantic salmon and never reach the weights of their seagoing relatives.

In appearance the landlocked salmon looks much like an Atlantic salmon except that it has larger eyes, longer fins and double-X black spots on its back. It is blue-green on its back and it has a reddish tint over its silvery sides.

Landlocked salmon are also called Sebago salmon, Sebago trout, Schoodic salmon, lake salmon, and ouananiche. The latter name is used in parts of Canada where this salmon is found.

Landlocked salmon are found mostly in Maine, New Hampshire, Vermont, northern New York State, and Canada. They have been introduced into many waters in these states and as far south as New Jersey. But they thrive best in the colder, northern lakes which are fairly large, deep, and contain plenty of smelt on which they feed.

But no matter where you find them, they rate as a top fresh-water game fish. They are tough, spectacular fighters guaranteed to provide plenty of thrills. It is also one of the largest game fish to be taken in many waters and makes fine eating.

In choosing tackle for landlocked salmon fishing many anglers rely on the fly rod—a medium- or heavy-weight rod from 8 to 9 feet long. It should have a fairly large reel to hold a fly line and about 100 yards of backing line. This can be used for trolling or casting. If you plan to do only trolling you actually don't need a fly line— you can fill your reel with 15- or 20-pound test monofilament line.

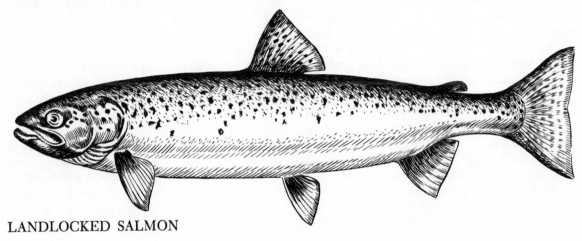

LANDLOCKED SALMON

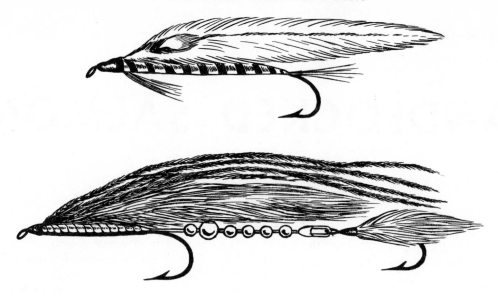

Streamers for landlocked salmon

However, more and more anglers are using spinning tackle both for trolling and casting lures. A medium fresh-water spinning rod and spinning reel filled with 6 or 8 pound test line can be used to troll lures or cast them from a boat or shore. A few anglers like to use bait-casting rods and reels for trolling or casting.

Lures used with a fly rod are mostly streamer or bucktail flies, wet flies, nymphs, and dry flies. The streamers used for trolling from boats are large and usually tied on tandem or double hooks. The most popular and effective streamers include the Black Ghost, Gray Ghost, Supervisor, Mickey Finn, Nine-Three, Green Ghost, Dark Tiger, Silver Doctor, Barred Lady, Barnes Special, and Green King.

Dry flies are used on certain days and certain waters when the landlocks feed on top. Such dry flies as the Grey Wulff, White Wulff, Green Drake, Gray Hackle with yellow body and the Black Gnat in sizes 8 to 14 should be carried for this fishing.

Lures for casting or trolling with spinning rods or bait-casting rods include the spoons, spinners, and small plugs.

Landlocked salmon are also caught on smelt or minnows which are sewn on a single or double hook rig. The smelt which is usually used is bent slightly so that it wobbles and flashes as it is trolled behind the boat. The smelt is trolled slowly anywhere from 50 to 80 feet behind the boat.

The best time of the year to catch landlocked salmon is as stated earlier, just when the ice breaks up on a lake. This may occur as early as April in the southern part of Maine and New York. But in the northern part of Maine and in Canada you may have to wait until May before this happens. When the smelt are moving into streams to spawn the landlocks congregate to feed on them at the inlets and along the shores. Later on, in late June, July, and August, when the water gets warm the landlocks go down into deeper water and are harder to reach and catch. In the fall in September and October the landlocks move into streams to spawn and good fishing can be had at times if the season is still open.

When the season first opens and the ice breaks up on the lake the weather is often raw and cold. But good landlocked salmon fishing can be had on such raw, wet, cold, windy days despite the weather. In fact, most landlocked salmon anglers agree that the days when the water is rough are better than when the lake is smooth and quiet. The landlocked salmon come right up on top when the water is rough. When the water is calm the fish go down and then deeper trolling is better. You can also have better luck on the calm days if you fish early in the

Landlocked salmon like these beauties are usually caught early in the spring soon after the ice is out. These were taken in Sebago Lake, Maine—a famous and productive spot for these fish. (MAINE DEPARTMENT OF ECONOMIC DEVELOPMENT)

morning and at dusk. If the water is choppy or rough you can take salmon during the middle of the day.

Look for landlocked salmon around the mouths of streams entering into the lake. Troll for them along rocky shorelines, ledges, and wherever there are sharp drop-offs into deeper water. Rocky points and shoals where they drop-off into deeper water are also good spots to try. Landlocks tend to gather and feed on the side or shore where the waves pile up. At other times they may be scattered all over the lake and are even caught in the middle of the lake. On certain occasions they can be seen chasing smelt or other small baitfish to the surface.

The most popular and productive method of catching landlocks is to troll streamer flies and lures such as spoons or spinners behind a boat. This is usually done with two or three rods and two men in a boat. Two fly rods are placed in rod holders attached to each corner of the stern. Then a spinning rod or bait-casting rod is placed in the middle. The streamers usually used on the fly rod are trailed from 40 to 60 feet behind the boat. The spinning rod or bait-casting rod with a spoon or spinner can be trolled much closer, about 20 to 30 feet from the stern. Landlocks are not boat shy but seem to be attracted by the wake of a moving boat.

In trolling, you will, of course, cover the hot spots where landlocks are believed to be present. Or you can follow the contour of the lake shore by weaving in and out. One man can cast toward shore from the moving boat. When the water is choppy no rod action is necessary to obtain strikes. But when the water is calm or when fish refuse to strike a straight trolled lure, you can impart rod action to tease the fish into striking. Raising and lowering the rod tip is one way—another way is by pulling back and forth on the line to make the lure dart forward, then drop back. You can also vary the speed of the boat to see which brings the most strikes.

Many expert anglers prefer to cast rather than troll for their fish in the early spring when the fish are on top. You can work the mouths of streams and the shoreline casting streamers with a fly rod. Anglers using spinning or bait-casting tackle can cast spinners and spoons. Your chances are increased if you can find landlocked

salmon feeding on smelt and chasing them to the surface.

Later on, during the summer and fall months, good fishing can sometimes be had for landlocked salmon with dry flies, wet flies, and nymphs. In lakes the dry fly is usually given some action by making it jump, shake, or skate on top. The best fishing in lakes with dry flies usually takes place early in the morning or evening when the salmon are feeding on insects.

Some of the best fishing with streamers, dry flies, wet flies, and nymphs takes place in streams when the landlocked salmon enter such waters. Then you can work the various flies in much the same manner as for trout, allowing them to float or drift through the pools, pockets, and runs.

During the hot summer months in most lakes, however, landlocked salmon go down deep and can only be caught by fishing with live bait or by deep trolling. This usually means using wire lines on fairly heavy tackle and trolling a series of spinners with baits such as smelt, minnows, or worms. Instead of the bait you can also use a small underwater plug or a spoon. Monel lines testing about 20 pounds can be used and you may have to let out anywhere from 60 to 200 feet to reach the ledges and spring holes where the salmon are found. You have to experiment with various lengths and speeds of trolling until you get a strike. It's a good idea to mark your line with quick-drying lacquer or nail polish when you do get a strike so that you can let out the same length of line and repeat.

But deep trolling doesn't give you the same thrills and fight from a landlocked salmon as surface fishing. When hooked on the top, a landlocked salmon is a fast, flashy scrapper who hits a lure hard, runs, leaps, twists, circles, and dives all around the boat. Many fish are lost during the fight or right at the boat itself. A big, wide-mouthed net is best when boating a salmon and even then great care must be taken. The safest procedure is to fight the fish as long as possible, until it turns over on its side—then net it *head* first.

Landlocked salmon don't grow as big as Atlantic salmon and usually range from 2 to 6 pounds. A 10- or 12-pounder is a big fish. The record taken on rod and reel is a 22½-pound

The larger, deeper lakes in Maine contain landlocked salmon. Trolling streamer flies with a fly rod is the most effective method of taking these great fighters. (MAINE DEVELOPMENT COMMISSION PHOTO BY FRENCH)

fish caught in Sebago Lake, Maine, on August 1, 1907, by Edward Blakely. Slightly bigger fish have been reported from Argentina where landlocked salmon have been introduced.

Landlocked salmon are found in Canada in New Brunswick, Ontario, and Quebec. In Maine, over 300 lakes have salmon with some of the best waters including Sebago Lake, Mooselookmeguntic Lake, Moosehead Lake, Grand Lake, Long Lake, Eagle Lake, Green Lake, Sebec Lake, Square Lake, Fish River chain of lakes, Rangeley Lakes, Kennebec River, and Union River. Vermont has such lakes as the Caspian, Memphremogog, Willoughby, Big Averill, and Seymour. New Hampshire has Lake Winnipesaukee, Sunapee, Merrymeeting, and Dan Hole ponds and the Connecticut chain of lakes. In New York State a few lakes in the Adirondack region contain landlocked salmon with Schroon Lake and Lake George the best known and most productive. In New Jersey, Mountain Lake has been stocked with landlocked salmon.

Chapter 7

BROWN TROUT

The brown trout is a relative newcomer to the American continent compared to the native brook trout and rainbow trout which were on the scene long before the white man or, for that matter, the Indians appeared. The first brown trout were sent to this country from Germany in 1883 by Herr F. Von Behr. At that time 80,000 brown trout eggs were sent to Fred Mather and arrived at New York's Cold Spring Harbor Hatchery on Long Island. Some of the brown trout eggs were forwarded to the Caledonia hatchery in New York State. During the following years additional shipments of eggs of a different variety of brown trout called the Loch Leven arrived from Scotland and England.

From the year 1886 the distribution of young brown trout expanded rapidly to various New York waters. Later other shipments of brown trout were sent to other states and Canada. Nowadays the brown trout is found in almost every state except those in the deep South where it is scarce or absent. Actually, the brown trout is an international fish, being found in most of Europe, parts of the Middle East, North and South Africa, North and South America, Asia, Australia, and New Zealand.

When brown trout first appeared in numbers in American waters they weren't welcomed with open arms by most trout fishermen. In fact, many protested violently that the brown trout was ugly, not too good to eat and not much of a fighter on the end of a line. They also said the brown trout was a cannibal that ate other trout and was responsible for the disappearance of the brook trout in eastern streams.

But as the years went by the genuine qualities of the brown trout have revealed themselves and today this immigrant is revered by countless fly fishermen. He's still not too popular a trout with the casual fisherman or the clumsy, unskilled novice. They'd rather fish for the rainbow trout or brook trout which are easier to catch. The brown trout is wild, wary, and soon learns to survive in hard-fished civilized streams and lakes. As the streams and rivers turn warmer and more polluted, conditions become unsuitable for brook trout and even rainbow trout. The result

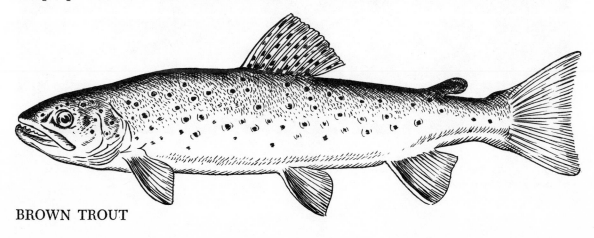

BROWN TROUT

Fly fishing for brown trout requires intense concentration and proper manipulation of the lure. Note how Larry Blaney fishing the Big Pine in Pennsylvania gathers slack line with his left hand. (PHOTO BY JOHNNY NICKLAS, PENNSYLVANIA FISH COMMISSION)

is that more and more waters end up containing mostly brown trout.

This situation is welcomed by the dry fly purists and serious trout anglers. To them the brown trout presents a challenge unmatched by other trout. He rises more readily to a dry fly than either the rainbow or brook trout. He is also more selective in his feeding and thus harder to fool with ordinary lures and baits. Brown trout are now found in many waters near large cities and towns where other trout are scarce or absent. Catching a brook trout or rainbow trout is considered fun and sport but catching a good-sized brown trout is considered an achievement.

At one time scientists used to differentiate between European brown trout, German brown trout, Loch Levens, and others, but today they are all lumped under the name of *Salmo trutta*. Anglers call it the brown trout or brownie.

The name indicates the color of the fish, which is usually some shade of brown. This may range from pale dirty yellow to olive-brown or greenish brown. These colors become lighter toward the belly which is creamy-white or yellowish. There are dark spots on the head, dorsal fin, and the back above the lateral line. Orange or reddish spots are often found along the sides. Brown trout which run to sea or live in lakes usually are bright silver. Large, old brown trout develop big heads and a hooked, undershot lower jaw.

Fly rods from short, 7-footers to long, heavy 9-footers are used for brown trout depending on the waters being fished and the lures being used. As a general rule for small streams, small fish and dry fly fishing, the shorter, lighter rods are best. For big waters, big fish, and for casting wet flies, streamers, and bucktails, the longer, heavier rods are best. Most anglers use a single-action fly reel. The smaller reels are filled with double-tapered fly lines for dry fly fishing, while the medium-sized and larger reels are filled with sinking fly lines or weight-forward fly lines to use with nymphs, wet flies, and streamers.

For casting lures and live baits a light or medium weight spinning rod can be used with a spinning reel. Here too, the lighter spin rods are best for small waters and small fish and for casting light lures. The medium-weight spinning rod is better for big waters, big fish, and heavier lures. Lines testing 2 to 4 pounds are best for the light outfits and small fish, while the heavier 4- to 8-pound test lines are used with heavier outfits for big fish.

Some brown trout are also caught on spin-casting, bait-casting, and cane and glass poles.

The angler who seeks brown trout with a fly rod has to carry a wider selection of flies than he needs for the other trouts. A wise old brownie that has been approached on many occasions or has been hooked and got away becomes "educated" and selective. Even the smaller brown trout will often demand a fly which matches closely those they are feeding on. Some of the more popular and tested dry flies which can be used for brown trout include the Adams, Light Cahill, Quill Gordon, Blue Dun, Black Gnat, Hendrickson, Light Blue Quill, White Miller, Royal Coachman, Ginger Variant, Ginger Quill, and Pale Evening Dun. The various bi-visibles and spiders are also good. Grasshopper imitations should also be carried during August and September when these insects are numerous. Sizes from 8 to 18 may be needed in dry flies.

In wet fly patterns brownies often go for the March Brown, Grey Miller, Cahill, Leadwing Coachman, and Gold Ribbed Hare's Ear. These should be carried in sizes from 8 to 14.

Nymphs take many brown trout early in the spring and throughout the year. There are many patterns on the market which can be used but those that match the nymphs found in the waters being fished are most effective.

An assortment of streamers and bucktails should also be carried when fishing for big brown trout which often feed on minnows. Here too, it's a good idea to use streamers which imitate the minnows and small fish found in the river or streams. Some of the proven bucktails and streamers are the Mickey Finn, Black Nose Dace, Brown and White, Black and White, Black Ghost, Gray Ghost, White Marabou, Black Marabou, and Yellow Marabou. These should be carried in hook sizes from 6 to 12.

When using spinning, spin-casting, or light bait-casting tackle various kinds of small lures should be carried. Most of these are actually made for bass fishing but the smaller, lighter sizes are also effective for trout. These include the different kinds of spinners, spoons, small underwater plugs, jigs, and plastic and rubber lures.

Which fly should I use? When fishing for brown trout you'd better find out what they want. Expert anglers usually carry a wide assortment of flies and change them often until they find the pattern and size the fish are hitting. (NEW YORK STATE DEPARTMENT OF COMMERCE)

Bait fishing for brown trout is done with such natural baits as earthworms, minnows, crayfish, frogs, and various land and water insects.

Brown trout can be caught during most of the trout fishing season but certain times are better than others. The bait fisherman and spinning angler usually do best early in the year during April and early May. This is also a good time for fishing streamers and bucktails as well as wet flies and nymphs. Later on from the middle of May till the end of June, the dry fly fishermen usually does best. But the farther north you go and the higher altitude you fish the better the fishing during the summer months. Many lakes and streams in our northernmost states and Canada provide good brown trout fishing in July and August. September is often a good month in many areas if the trout season is still open.

Early in the spring when the water is still cold your best fishing will be during the middle of the day. This is also true in the late fall when the water turns cold. Later on, as the water turns warmer and insects hatch more in the evening your best fishing will be in the late afternoon and evening. During the hot summer months early morning and dusk or night provide the best fishing. In fact, big brown trout are noted for their night feeding habits during the summer months.

The best way to locate brown trout or any trout for that matter is to live by the stream and spend many hours observing the fish and where they hide and feed. Brown trout especially are noted for their habit of choosing a spot and staying there. Big ones, particularly, will take over a pool and chase away or eat the smaller ones. Because of this, fishing a pool will often be a waste of time if the only resident is a big, wise brownie. But other pools may contain several good-sized fish and these can be sought at the heads and tails of the pool and even in the deeper water.

Brown trout like shade or cover over their heads during the daytime. So look for them under rocks, logs, banks, roots of trees, bridges, and any other spot which provides cover and safety. Brown trout are usually found in the slower moving stretches such as shallow pools and runs. But during the summer they may be in fairly fast water especially if there are big rocks or boulders with deep pockets in between. A brown trout likes to lie in front of such a rock, boulder, or other obstruction which splits the current. In the evening, brown trout may come out of their hiding places and venture into shallow water at the heads and tails of pools and along the shore to feed.

Of course, the easy way to locate brown trout is to actually see them lying in the water on the bottom or rising for flies which are hatching. Sometimes you'll see only dimples or wakes made by feeding fish.

Once the fish is located or a specific spot is suspected of harboring a trout, caution must be observed in approaching the fish. In shallow water and small streams, especially, you must keep out of sight, avoid casting a shadow and move as slowly as possible. Try to avoid wading and fish from shore if possible. If not, move as carefully as you can so that you don't create a disturbance.

Dry fly fishing is most effective when flies are hatching and fish are feeding on them. Or when trout are in a feeding location and are waiting to see what the current brings their way. During a hatch it is important to match the size, color, and general outline of the natural insects they are feeding on. As a general rule the larger flies are better early in the year and the smaller ones later on, when the water is low and clear.

Proper presentation of the dry fly is important and it should be dropped lightly and accurately a few feet in front of the fish so that it drifts naturally with the current. The line should float but the leader should sink. The slack line should be gathered with your left hand but not so fast as to cause the line to pull on the fly. Drag should be avoided because it gives the fly an unnatural movement and speed. In most dry fly fishing you cast upstream and slightly across. But if you see the fish or pinpoint the location of one you can cast a few feet above it so that the fly drifts over it. You can also cast downstream if standing directly above the fish's position. In this case plenty of slack is needed to allow the fly to drift down naturally.

In wet fly fishing for brown trout you can cast across and slightly upstream and let the fly sink toward the bottom. Here too, it should drift naturally with no pull or drag. Follow the general direction of the fly with your rod tip and watch for a strike. You may feel a slight tug or pause

When you catch a brown trout this size you can be proud of your accomplishment. Brown trout are warier than most other trout. This one came from the Sandy River in Maine. (MAINE DEPARTMENT OF ECONOMIC DEVELOPMENT)

but most of the time you have to depend on other signs, such as a flash of a fish underwater or the pull on the leader or fly line. Some anglers attach a dry fly above the wet fly and watch this to indicate a bite. After a wet fly has finished its drift and you want to retrieve it do so with short, quick jerks. Often a trout will grab it as it moves upstream against the current.

Nymphs are fished somewhat like wet flies in that you cast upstream or across and let them drift naturally with the current. At the end of the drift let the nymph pause and rise toward the surface. Then you can retrieve it in short jerks. Here too, detecting a strike is often difficult and you have to develop a sort of sixth sense to enable you to set the hook at the right moment. Nymphs are deadly early in the spring and throughout the season because brown trout and the other trout often feed on the natural nymphs.

For the larger trout you can't beat streamers and bucktails. These are usually best early in the spring and in the summer right after a shower or rain. But they are also good early in the morning and evening when brownies are chasing minnows in the shallows or tails of pools. One way to fish them is to cast quartering upstream and let them drift down with the current. The line should be fairly slack. When it reaches the end of the drift let it flutter a few seconds, then bring it in with spurts or darts. The idea is to simulate a crippled or frightened minnow. Try different speeds from slow to fast and different

depths from shallow to deep and short jerks or long sweeps. In pools and lakes you can work them near the surface or let them sink deep and then bring them to the top in slow, short jerks.

The spinning rod is an effective weapon for big brown trout particularly on the larger streams, rivers, and lakes. With such a rod you can reach spots such as runs, pools, pockets, overhanging banks where brown trout may be lying, or feeding. Such lures as spinners, spoons, jigs, and small plugs can be cast at almost any angle and worked at varying speeds. The sinking lures can be retrieved near the surface fast or allowed to sink toward the bottom and retrieved in a slower, erratic manner.

More brown trout have probably been caught on an earthworm or night crawler than any other natural bait. This is especially true during the spring of the year, but a skillfully fished worm will take big brown trout throughout the year. You can fish the worm with a fly rod or spinning rod, but whichever tackle is used try to drift the worm deep and as naturally as possible into spots where trout may be lying. In slow to medium water you don't need a sinker, but faster water may call for some split-shot on the leader.

A minnow sewn on a single or double hook is often deadly for big brown trout. The minnow usually has a slight curve and is cast across stream and allowed to drift and sink toward the bottom, then is retrieved slowly with short pulls so that it wobbles and darts and flashes. Split

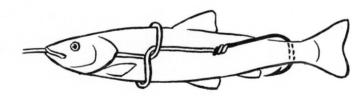

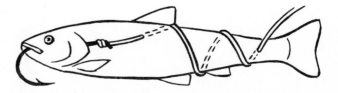

Two ways to sew a minnow on hook for big trout

shot are often added on the leader about 18 or 20 inches ahead of the minnow to provide weight for casting and allow the bait to sink in the faster runs and pools. It also lets the minnow rise when pulled, then sink down when you stop the retrieve to give it a crippled action.

Brown trout aren't spectacular fighters although they'll occasionally leap out of the water. Usually they prefer to slug it out below the surface and try to snag your leader or line around a rock or log. Big ones have the weight to give you plenty of trouble but after the first long run or two they can be handled more easily.

In the smaller streams brown trout will run about a pound to 3 or 4 pounds in weight. In larger rivers and lakes they'll run up to 8 or 10 pounds or more. Quite a few fish around the 20- to 25-pound mark have been taken on rod and reel. One of the largest in this country was the 26-pound 2-ounce brown trout taken in May 1958 at Dale Hollow Dam, Tennessee, by George Langston. One of the biggest brown trout on record is the 39½-pound fish caught by W. Muir in Loch Awe, Scotland.

The small- or medium-sized brown trout make pretty good eating. They have a firm, pinkish flesh and those from clear, cold streams are delicious. The larger ones are somewhat tougher but can still be eaten. However, if you catch a real big trout save it and have it mounted or at least photographed. Because it may be a long time before you get another one.

Chapter 8

BROOK TROUT

When the first white men settled in North America the only trout they found in the East was the brook trout. This colorful trout was the true "native" and the only one known to the first settlers. Up until the time the rainbow trout and brown trout were introduced into eastern waters the angler who went trout fishing caught only brook trout.

The brook trout was a great favorite of these early trout fishermen. Abundant in almost every river, stream, brook, and many lakes and ponds, it provided both sport and food. Early accounts tell of the wonderful brook trout fishing in many areas in New England, New York, and other states. The brook trout ranged in those days from Labrador west to Saskatchewan south through the Alleghenies to northern Georgia. Then he was introduced in the West from California to Alaska.

Today the brook trout is still a popular fish in those areas where it is fairly plentiful. It is the most co-operative of the trouts, feeding on a wide variety of foods and almost always willing to take a properly presented lure or bait. The brook trout is usually caught in scenic, beautiful, wild streams and rivers.

Unfortunately brook trout waters are becoming scarce and those that remain are often in remote areas which are difficult to reach. With the advance of civilization and growth of cities,

BROOK TROUT

Brook trout are often found in many of our northern lakes. Here an angler leads the fish into the net after it is played out. (NEW HAMPSHIRE STATE PHOTO BY DICK SMITH)

towns, farms, factories, lumbering and the accompanying pollution, and siltation, the waters suitable for brook trout are becoming more and more scarce. Now these fish are mainly confined to the wilderness areas, mountain brooks and ponds, and the upper reaches and feeder streams. Of course, hatcheries keep producing millions of brook trout for the "put-and-take" fishing practiced in many states. But most serious trout fishermen want the natural, wild brook trout and leave the mass production product for the casual trout fisherman.

Brook trout have been called Eastern brook trout, speckled trout, native trout, mountain trout, red trout, brookies, and squaretails. The brook trout isn't considered a true trout but belongs to the char family like the lake trout and Dolly Varden trout.

Anyone who has seen the brook trout in its fall spawning colors will admit that it is one of the prettiest of trouts. The back is usually blue-green or gray-green or bronze-green. There are lighter wormlike markings on the back and sides up to the lateral line. The sides have red dots outlined with blue. The fins have dark bands and are edged with pink blending into white. In small brooks, deep forests, and some Canadian rivers and lakes the brook trout is very dark all over. Those that run to the sea turn silvery, but soon revert to the original colors when in fresh water.

Brook trout can be caught on the same fishing outfits and tackle as the brown trout. Fly rods, of course, are best for casting the various dry and wet flies. Lures can be used with bait-casting, spinning, and spin-casting rods and reels.

Brook trout, especially in wilderness waters, often go for the more colorful, gaudier wet fly patterns. You can use the Parmachene Belle, Silver Doctor, Red Ibis, Royal Coachman, Montreal, Grizzly King, Professor, Black Gnat, and McGinty. Sizes No. 6 to 12 can be carried.

In dry flies the Black Gnat, Royal Coachman, White Wulff, Grey Wulff, Light Cahill, Dark Cahill, and Quill Gordon are good. You can also carry some of the spiders and bi-visibles. Sizes No. 10 to 18 in dry flies should be carried.

Nymphs such as the stone fly, may fly, and the gray fur-bodied nymphs are also good at times.

For the larger brook trout in big rivers and lakes bucktails and streamers such as the Red and White, Mickey Finn, Black Nosed Dace, White Marabou, and Edson Tiger Dark are a good assortment.

With the spinning and other casting outfits you can use such lures as spoons, spinners, and small plugs.

Brook trout are one of the easiest trout to catch on natural baits such as worms, minnows, grasshoppers, crickets, and nymphs.

Brook trout start feeding early in the spring soon after the ice is out and April, May, and June are usually good months. In the northern lakes and rivers in Maine and Canada you can sometimes have pretty good fishing in July and August but in more southern waters the summer months are not too good.

Brook trout prefer the cool, clean, turbulent waters in streams and rivers. In small streams look for them under undercut banks, submerged brush, logs, tree roots, log jams, behind rocks and ledges, in rapids and under waterfalls. They usually like to lie behind a rock, log or other obstruction. During the warmer months they may be in the deeper pools of rivers, around spring holes or the mouths of brooks. Many brook trout will move into the brooks themselves. In lakes, also, they will be around spring holes or where the cool brooks and rivers enter into the lake.

In certain Atlantic coastal streams the brook trout will migrate to sea, live there in salt water for a few years then return to the stream to spawn. These fish often reach a good size and provide excellent sport.

The brook trout is mostly an underwater feeder and can often be caught on wet flies fished slowly under the surface. The wet flies can be cast across and slightly upstream and slack line should be kept under control. You can drift the fly naturally, then retrieve it in short jerks. If a shallow-running fly doesn't work let it sink to the bottom and keep it working deep. Nymphs can be worked in the same way to attract trout.

When brook trout are feeding on a hatch of insects on top they'll also take a dry fly in streams and lakes. The fly should be drifted naturally on the river or stream with the current over the rising fish.

Freshly caught brook trout are pretty and colorful fish. They also make delicious eating. (NEW YORK STATE DEPARTMENT OF COMMERCE)

Streamers and bucktails are often effective for large brook trout in big rivers and lakes. They may feed on smelt or other small fish running up a stream to spawn and any streamers or bucktails resembling these baitfish are best. Give them an erratic, hesitant retrieve and try them at different depths from top to bottom.

Some big trout are also taken at times on lures such as small spoons, weighted spinners and underwater plugs. Here too, the lures which resemble the small fish prevalent in the waters being fished are best. Such lures can also be used for trolling on the larger lakes and rivers.

Live bait anglers find the ordinary garden worm a fine bait for brook trout especially in the spring of the year. At that time of year the trout will be hugging bottom and the worm should be drifted deep to reach them. The worm used for brook trout should be hooked through the middle and drifted along the edges of the fast water, under overhanging banks, around sunken trees and logs and in deep holes and pockets. Follow the drift of the worm with your rod and allow plenty of slack line for a natural drift. When a bite is felt wait a few seconds, then set the hook. The larger trout in lakes can sometimes be caught on live minnows, small fish, crayfish, and frogs. Insects such as grasshoppers and crickets can also be used for brook trout and are especially effective on the smaller meadow brooks.

A wild, good-sized brookie in fast water puts up a strong, stubborn battle. They rarely leap out of the water like the rainbow or even the brown trout at times. And they are not noted for making long runs. But they usually bore deep, twist, roll, and try to foul your line around a tree root, rock, or log.

Cool, mountain streams and brooks like this often contain brook trout. They like to lie in the foamy, white water under waterfalls, behind rocks, or other obstructions. (VERMONT DEVELOPMENT DEPARTMENT)

Unfortunately, most of the brook trout caught are small fish rarely more than 10 or 12 inches long. In some tiny brooks and mountain streams they are full-grown at 7 or 8 inches. However, in the more remote, wilderness areas in large rivers and lakes they are often taken up to 7 or 8 pounds. The world record on rod and reel is the 14½-pound brook trout taken by Dr. W. J. Cook on the Nipigon River, Ontario, Canada, July 1916.

A wild, fresh-caught brook trout makes delicious eating. The flavor and texture cannot be matched by the other trouts. The best brook trout fishing spots are in the Canadian provinces of Ontario, Manitoba, Quebec, New Brunswick, Nova Scotia, and in Labrador. In the United States they are most plentiful in our northern states with Maine outstanding. They have also been stocked in many of the mountain lakes and streams in the West.

Chapter 9

RAINBOW TROUT

The spectacular rainbow trout is one of the most popular trout with fishermen whether caught by fly-casting, spin-casting, trolling, or bait fishing. It is one of the most widely distributed of the trouts, being found from Alaska to California, throughout our northern states, in Canada and Europe, Asia, Africa, Australia, New Zealand, and South America.

Rainbow trout have been called California trout, Pacific trout, salmon trout, Western rainbow, and steelhead. The steelhead is a rainbow trout that goes to sea or into large lakes and then returns to the rivers to spawn. (See the chapter on steelhead for details on how to catch the sea-going rainbow trout.)

A rainbow trout is a colorful and beautiful fish when first removed from the water. The back is usually greenish or bluish shading into silvery green on the sides. The whole upper surface of the body, head, fins, and tail are covered

with small dark spots. A wide band of crimson or pink runs along the lateral line from head to tail. This stripe is most evident in large mature fish and males at breeding time. The female rainbow trout may lack this pink stripe and appear plain silvery. The rainbows that live in large bodies of water often turn dark blue on the back and silvery on the sides.

You can use the same tackle to catch rainbow trout as the outfits mentioned in detail in the chapter on brown trout. However, for the bigger rainbows on larger rivers and in big lakes you can use somewhat heavier fly rods, bait-casting, spinning and spin-casting outfits than for the smaller fish.

The fly rod angler will find that rainbow trout will take many of the same patterns as the brown trout or brook trout. In dry flies he can carry the Grizzly Sedge, Green Sedge, Quill Gordon, Light Cahill, Ginger Quill, Adams, Fanwing

RAINBOW TROUT

Trolling in cool mountain lakes is a good way to take rainbow trout. Small plugs, spoons, spinners, streamers, and wet flies can all be used. (MERCURY OUTBOARD MOTORS)

This 29¾-pound Kamloops rainbow was taken in Lake Pend Oreille, Idaho, famous for its giant trout. (IDAHO DE-PARTMENT OF COMMERCE AND DEVELOPMENT)

Royal Coachman, Hendrickson, and the Black Gnat. The various bi-visibles, spiders, and variants are also good at times. Sizes from No. 10 to 18 can be carried in dry flies.

In wet flies you can stock such patterns as the Brown Sedge, Green Sedge, Coachman, Royal Coachman, Alexandria, Skykomish Sunrise, Parmachene Belle, McGinty, Gray Hackle Yellow, Black Gnat, Mosquito, and the Wooly Worm. Here sizes from No. 8 to 16 can be carried.

Nymphs are very good in low clear water and in many lakes. The different patterns used for other trout will work for rainbows too. In mountain lakes nymphs with fur "dubbing" bodies are good. Sizes No. 8, 10, and 12 are favorites.

Streamers and bucktails which will take rainbow trout include the Mickey Finn, Red and White, Black Nosed Dace, Gray Ghost, Supervisor, and Black Ghost.

Shrimp flies and grasshopper imitations should also be carried in certain areas and at certain times of the year.

For use with a spinning, spin-casting, or bait-casting rod the various lures such as spinners, spoons, jigs, and small plugs are good. They are especially effective on the larger rivers and lakes for big rainbow trout and early in the season when the water is cold.

Rainbow trout are also caught on various natural baits such as salmon eggs, worms, crayfish, hellgrammites, grubs, and minnows. Where salmon eggs are illegal anglers often use substitutes such as red yarn on a hook, cooked tapioca dyed red, Vaseline formed in the shape of an egg, and similar imitations.

Rainbow trout fishing is usually best early in the spring during April and May when the fish run up rivers to spawn. Another good period is during September, October, and November when big rainbow trout return to the rivers from the larger lakes. But small rainbow trout can be caught during the summer months in many waters. There is often good fishing in Canada and Alaska during the hot months.

The time of day when fishing is best will depend on the season and water temperatures. Early in the spring and late in the fall the fishing is good during the middle of the day. And in the colder climates and high mountain lakes it is also good during the middle of the day. In warmer climates and during the summer months early morning or evening hours are usually better.

Rainbow trout like the faster portions of rivers and streams. Thus you'll often find them in the rapids, riffles, fast glides and runs, and in the white water at the heads and tails of pools and under waterfalls. In lakes, rainbows will gather at the mouths of brooks or rivers, and around spring holes during the summer months. In clear, mountain lakes you can often spot rainbows cruising near shore.

Rainbows are pretty good dry fly fish and will often rise to the surface to feed on hatching flies. Then you can drift a dry fly in the same manner as described for brown trout in the section dealing with that fish. Dry flies will also take rainbows in lakes when they are feeding on hatches of flies in the evening.

To fish a nymph in these lakes use a sinking fly line and let the nymphs sink deep. Then retrieve it in short jerks toward the surface. However, if you actually sight a fish you can cast the nymph or a wet fly ahead of it. In crystal-clear lakes this means casting a fairly long line and dropping the fly at least 6 or 7 feet ahead of the fish in order not to spook them.

The lures such as spoons, spinners, and small underwater plugs are most effective early in the year and for the larger rainbows in rivers and lakes. These are cast across stream and upstream and are allowed to tumble and drift and sink in the current. When they reach a point downstream from the angler they can be retrieved erratically against the current. In lakes they can be cast and retrieved at various depths.

Trolling is a good way to take rainbow trout on the larger rivers and most lakes. You can use wet flies, streamers, and nymphs on a sinking fly line at a rowing speed. Extra rod action or pulls on the line can be imparted to give the flies a more lifelike action. During the summer months when the rainbow trout are down deep in most lakes, troll in deep water with a lot of line out. One of the most effective lures for this trolling is a series of spinners in front of a worm or minnow. You can also use spoons, weighted spinners, or underwater plugs. Early in the spring, late in the fall, and early in the morning or late in the evening, troll close to shore. Big rainbows often come into the shallows then to feed on insects and minnows.

Bait fishing is very effective for rainbow trout in many streams and rivers. Anywhere from one to five salmon eggs on a hook can be used where this is legal. Night crawlers or garden worms are also good especially in the spring of the year. These baits should be cast upstream and across and allowed to drift along the bottom with the current. Sometimes a few split-shot or a small pencil sinker is added above the baited hook to keep it down in fast water.

When hooked the rainbow becomes a fighting demon on the end of a line. It will make long runs, leap out of the water, often, and move with a speed which puts other trouts to shame. Fight them on a fairly tight line because if they gain too much slack, they may throw the hook.

In the smaller streams and lakes, rainbows will average from 1 to 5 pounds, but in the larger rivers and lakes they often reach a heavy weight. The rainbows that have access to a big body of water with plenty of minnows or other fish for food will grow to 15 or 20 pounds. The Kamloops form of rainbow found mostly in Idaho and British Columbia reach even a bigger size. The rod and reel record is 37 pounds and was caught in Lake Pend Oreille, Idaho, on November 25, 1947. Many other fish in the 30-pound class have been taken from these waters. Even bigger Kamloops rainbows have been reported from British Columbia where fish going over 40 pounds have been trapped by the game commission for eggs. There are also two huge Kamloops rainbows of 48 and 52½ pounds mentioned as being taken from Jewel Lake, British Columbia, in 1931 and 1933.

Rainbow trout taken from wilderness streams and lakes make excellent eating. The hatchery trout are not as good but after they live in a lake or stream for a few months they improve.

Rainbow trout are found in so many waters in this country, Canada, and Alaska that it is impossible to list even a few of the best waters. The best fishing and the largest number of fish are found in our northern states, such as Washington, Oregon, California, Utah, Montana, Michigan, Wisconsin, Minnesota, New York, Vermont, New Hampshire, and Maine. Many waters in Canada offer fine rainbow trout fishing with British Columbia tops for big fish. And the rainbow trout fishing in Alaska is fabulous. In South America, Chile and Peru have some monster rainbow trout in their mountain lakes and rivers.

Rainbow trout like fast water and put up a spectacular fight when caught on light tackle. (MICHIGAN TOURIST COUNCIL)

Chapter 10

STEELHEAD

The steelhead is a rainbow trout which migrates down a coastal river to the sea, spends a few years there and then returns up the river to spawn. Anglers along the Pacific Coast from California to Alaska have no Atlantic salmon in those waters but are perfectly content with the steelhead as a substitute. In fact, both fish are very similar in appearance, habits, and fighting ability and it is difficult to determine which is superior.

More anglers fish for steelhead than for Atlantic salmon because they are much more numerous and are found in many rivers. Most of the steelhead rivers are open to the public and the fishing seasons are long. And you are not restricted to the kind of tackle you can use as is the case with Atlantic salmon where only fly rods are allowed.

All this makes the steelhead highly popular with Pacific Coast anglers who seek this fish in rain, snow, sleet, and freezing weather during the winter months. But although steelhead are much more numerous than Atlantic salmon they are not an easy fish to catch. They offer a challenge to most anglers whether novice or expert.

It takes skill to locate steelhead, cast, present the bait or lure, then hook and fight them successfully. In the rushing rivers where they are found they are real tackle-busters and you can consider yourself lucky if you land more than half of the steelhead you hook.

A steelhead looks like a rainbow trout except that it may be bigger, longer, more streamlined and different in color when it first comes in from the sea. When fresh from the sea a steelhead as its name implies has a steel-blue or greenish back, silvery sides and some dark spots on the back and tail. After it has been in fresh water for a while it reverts back to the original rainbow trout colors.

Steelhead are caught with various types of fishing outfits from dainty fly rods to heavy surf-fishing rods. Years ago, the most popular rod was a long bait-casting or two-handed rod which was used with a bait-casting reel or small salt-water revolving reel for drift fishing. Such outfits are still used but most have been replaced by spinning rods ranging from 7 to 8½ feet long. These are used with good-sized spinning reels filled with lines testing from 8 to 20 pounds.

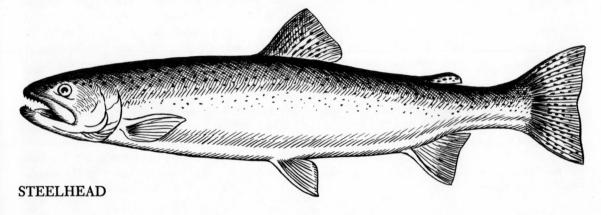

STEELHEAD

These winter-run steelhead were taken from the Green River, Washington. Those caught at this time of year run bigger than the summer fish. (WASHINGTON STATE DEPARTMENT OF GAME)

Even longer spinning rods similar to surf rods with heavy salt-water spinning reels are used for long casts at the mouths of rivers where steelhead gather.

For fly fishing a good, powerful rod from 8 to 9½ feet long is usually used. A weight-forward sinking line is used with this rod when fishing wet flies. Tapered leaders of 9 or 12 feet tapering down to 8-, 6-, or 4-pound test are attached to the fly line.

Since most steelhead fishing is done from shore by wading in the river to reach the hot spots a pair of waist-high waders is almost a must. However, some spots can also be fished with hip boots. Both waders and hip boots should have felt soles or hobnails to help keep your footing in fast water.

The angler who prefers to use artificial lures for steelhead will get some spoons in various sizes, colors, and weights. Weighted spinners are also good for casting and probing the bottom where steelhead lie. The cherry bobber spinner which has a balsa body to keep it from sinking is used with a sinker and is often deadly for steelies. Various types of jigs can also be used to get down deep. Underwater plugs are also used mostly with sinkers in order to reach the bottom. Then there are the flies made from yarn which are tied around a hook. These are usually a bright fluorescent color, particularly yellow, orange, or red.

For the fly-rod angler there are many wet flies which can be used including many of the standard trout patterns. There are also special patterns tied especially for steelhead. A good assortment will include the Royal Coachman, Silver Doctor, Gray Hackle, Queen Bess, Van Luven, Skykomish Sunrise, Polar Shrimp, Umpqua, Silver Ant, Thor, Golden Demon, Bobbie Dun, Harger's Orange, and Paint Brush. Atlantic salmon flies will also take steelhead at times. Wet flies in sizes No. 4, 6, and 8 are usually the most effective.

When steelhead take dry flies you can use such patterns as the Grey Wulff, Black Wulff, March Brown, Adams, Royal Coachman, Light Cahill, and Pink Lady in sizes No. 6, 8, 10, and 12.

Steelhead are also caught on natural baits such as salmon eggs which are fished in clusters on a hook. Fresh eggs taken from a female steelhead are also very good. These are made up into clusters in tiny bags of thin maline netting. Three-inch squares of this material are used with the eggs placed in the center and the corners gathered together and then tied with a thread. Sometimes a large single salmon egg or two or three of them are used on a single hook. Steelhead will also take crayfish tails or night crawlers fished near the bottom.

The key to success in steelhead fishing is the timing of your fishing trip to coincide with the run of fish up the river. Since this may vary from river to river and from year to year it requires constant checking. Some rivers have only one main run of fish such as the summer run which may start in April in some rivers or as late as August and September in others. Other rivers may have a summer run and then later on a winter run which may begin in October or later and last until February and March on some rivers. On still other rivers there are continuous runs of fish from early spring to winter. Before planning a trip it's a good idea to get in touch with someone who is right on the river and can tell you if the steelhead are running.

On short rivers the runs may only last a few weeks with the fish moving rapidly. On the period of time with different portions of the longer rivers, the runs spread out over a greater river producing fast fishing as the steelhead move upstream. Here you have to follow the fish or intercept them if you want to catch them. Large stretches of the river may be barren of fish or contain only a few strays while other sections will provide good fishing.

Even when the fish are in the river there is no guarantee of good fishing. A sudden storm, prolonged rain, or drop in water temperature may put a stop to the fishing. It has been found that when the water temperature is below 39 degrees Fahrenheit the steelhead are inactive and feed little. Also, a rapidly rising river which becomes discolored is a poor time to fish. But after the river starts to clear and when the water is a milky green or blue is a good time to fish. After a heavy rain the upper portions of a river clear first, then the lower portions. It may take two, three, or more days for the fishing to return to normal in some rivers. In others it may take several days or a week or two before it pays to go fishing. That is why the natives or those anglers living near the river have the advantage. They can wait and watch the river to choose the best fishing periods. But anglers some distance from the river can check the weather reports to find out if it rained there recently or if any rains are expected.

During the summer you can fish for steelhead during the day but if it is sunny and hot your chances are best early in the morning and again in the evening. During the winter months if the weather and water are cold you can fish during the midafternoon when the water may warm up a bit.

Even after you arrive on a river and are assured that the fish are present there is another important hurdle to overcome. You have to locate the fish in the river itself so that you can present the bait or lure to them. If you have fished the river before and know the locations and spots where the fish like to lie or rest this is not a big problem. But if you are fishing a strange river or are a beginner then you have your work cut out for you.

The main point to keep in mind is that steelhead are usually found in "holding" or "resting" spots where they are protected from the main force of the current. So in a riffle or rapid they will be found along the edges of the fast water at the head or tail of the run. If there are boulders or rocks, look for the fish in front, behind, or along the sides of such obstructions. Along the banks of a river they may lie behind rock out-

Cluster of salmon eggs held by leader loop

Steelhead rig for drift fishing

croppings, rock ledges, undercut banks, over-hanging trees, or behind logs and driftwood. In pools look for them at the tails or heads rather than in the deeper, quieter sections. Pools should be fished from the shallow side with casts being made toward the deeper side.

Most expert steelhead anglers study their favorite river during the low water periods. They memorize and pinpoint the location of every boulder, rock, log, hole, depression, and obstruction which may harbor a steelhead later when the river rises. Then they can cast their lure or bait into these spots even though they cannot be seen below the surface. Once they take some fish from these spots they know they can return and catch some more as new fish replace those which have been caught or have moved upstream.

The method usually used to catch steelhead is by drifting a natural bait such as salmon eggs or an artificial lure such as a spinner or spoon close to the bottom. A special rig is made up for this by making use of a three-way swivel. A leader from 18 to 36 inches long is tied to one eye of the swivel. A hook is tied to the end of the leader. This can be a size such as No. 4 or No. 2 for clusters of salmon eggs. For a single hook a small No. 10 hook is used. To the other eye of the three-way swivel a short 6-inch dropper leader is tied and to this you attach a pencil sinker from ¼ to an ounce or more depending on the depth being fished and the strength of the current. The line is tied to the remaining eye on the swivel. (See illustration.)

This rig is used for drift fishing and the proven technique is to cast across the current or up-stream and let the bait drift downstream on a tight line so that the sinker bounces bottom at all times. That's the main secret—keep the sinker rolling or bouncing on the bottom so that the bait passes through the resting or holding spots where steelhead are lying. You keep taking up slack line, raise and lower the rod tip, feed some line as the situation demands, always on the alert for the slightest pause or nibble indicating a bite. Then you raise the rod tip smartly to set the hook. You may be fouled on the bottom or into a log, but you still have to strike at every indication of a bite.

Although natural baits, such as salmon eggs and worms are used a lot, artificial lures such as spinners, spoons, and plugs can also be used for drift fishing. Natural baits are usually best when the water is high and somewhat roily. Lures work better when the water is clear and low. Lures can often be worked along the bottom without the help of a sinker. Here too, you can cast from the bank upstream and across and let the current take the lure down and give it action. Other times you can reel the lure slowly and even give it additional jerks with the rod tip. If you can wade above a good holding spot you can let your lure down with the current and keep working it back and forth in a small area.

On certain rivers, the best spots are reached by boat and here steelhead are also taken by drift fishing and trolling. If you can hold the boat in one spot or anchor, you can let your bait or lure move down with the current into holes or other spots where steelhead may be lying. Here you may also need a sinker to get the bait or lure down close to the bottom.

Some steelhead rivers are wide, sluggish, and often muddy, and here still fishing or "plunking" is the most effective method. A plunker chooses a spot and stays there most of the time. He casts out his salmon eggs, worms, or crayfish tails and lets the bait rest on or near the bottom. Then he puts his rod in a holder or forked stick and sits down to await a bite. He uses fairly heavy bait-casting or spinning rod and lines testing 15 to 20 pounds.

For real sport nothing beats hooking and fighting a steelhead on a fly rod. Unfortunately, this fishing is restricted to certain rivers and certain seasons. It is most effective during the summer or fall months and when the water is low and clear. Wet flies are used much in the same manner as when trout fishing. You cast upstream and allow the fly to sink close to the bottom, take up slack line. Usually, the fly is allowed to drift without any rod action but other times added motion can be provided by moving the fly in short jerks. At times, you can also catch steelhead on dry flies on the surface. This usually takes place in the summer or early fall when insects are hatching and steelies are feeding on

them. The late afternoon or evening hours are usually best for this fishing. Here too, the fly is allowed to drift naturally with the current, but steelhead have been known to take a fly which was dragged or skittered along the surface.

Once you hook a steelhead on any kind of tackle you can look forward to a fast, spectacular fight. The smaller fish will leap out of the water again and again. Steelies of all sizes will make long, fast, powerful runs often forcing you to follow them downstream in a strong current. The safest way to land a steelhead is to beach him on a sloping rock, gravel, or sand bar. When fishing from a boat a wide-mouthed net or gaff can be used.

Steelhead caught during the summer run range in weight from 2 to 8 pounds. The winter fish are much larger often going up to 15 or 20 pounds. A few up to 30 pounds are taken each year and they have been caught up to 36 pounds in weight.

In California, steelhead are found in such rivers as the Klamath, Trinity, Eel, Sacramento, Russian, and Smith. In Oregon, there are many rivers such as the Rogue, Umpqua, Deschutes, Coquille, Siletz, Siuslaw, Sandy, Alsea, Wilson, Big Nestucca, and the Columbia. In Washington there's also the Columbia and Duckabush, Kalama, Stillaguamish, Snoqualmie, Washougal, Wind, Quinault, Dosewallips, Green, Lewis, Puyallup, Skagit, Skykomish, Nisqually, and Chehalis. In British Columbia such rivers as the Frazer, Kispiox, Cowichan, Skeena, Cooper, and Sustut offer great steelhead fishing. On Vancouver Island, the famed Campbell River produces many steelhead.

Of course, there are many other rivers and streams in the areas listed which may have steelhead runs. Some may be good one year and a flop the next. Some may be blocked by sand bars which form at the mouth and prevent the steelhead from entering. Heavy winter rains often open these rivers to the steelhead. For the latest information on the rivers it's a good idea to contact local fishermen, sporting goods stores, outdoor writers on newspapers, or pay a visit to the river yourself to see firsthand if fish are being caught.

Great sport can be had with a fly rod fishing for steelhead during the summer and early fall. Wet flies in sizes 4, 6, and 8 are more effective but at times steelhead will also take dry flies. (CANADIAN TRAVEL BUREAU)

Chapter 11

LAKE TROUT

The lake trout is one of those fishes which isn't too well known to many anglers and not too popular as a game fish. Mostly because they are found in a limited range and good fishing for them usually takes place during seasons when few anglers are on the water. So only a small percentage of fresh-water anglers have had first-hand experience with lake trout or have caught them. But for those anglers who live in areas where lake trout are found and who spend time seeking them there is fine sport to be had with these large fish.

The lake trout is a char like the Dolly Varden trout and brook trout. It is also called the Mackinaw, togue, Great Lakes trout, forktail trout, gray trout, salmon trout, namaycush, and laker.

In color it varies from gray or light green to brown and black. The whole body is covered with lighter, irregular spots. The belly is cream-colored or white. It has a large head, large mouth with strong teeth and forked tail.

Originally the lake trout was found from Labrador to Alaska, through the Great Lakes and in northern New England. But it has been introduced into many other northern states and as far south as Connecticut and New York.

When lake trout are on the surface or in shallow water you can use bait-casting, spinning, and spin-casting rods and reels to catch them. Some anglers even use the heavier fly rods for casting or trolling. But when they are in deep water heavier fishing tackle such as musky rods and reels, salt-water rods and reels are in order. Since much of this trolling in deep water is done with solid wire lines you need a strong salt-water type reel with a metal spool holding up to 500 or 600 feet of line. Monel stainless steel lines in 20- and 30-pound test are popular for this fishing. You can also use monofilament lines and braided lines and lead-core lines for trolling but then you must use heavy sinkers or trolling weights to get the lure down.

The lures used are spoons of various types up

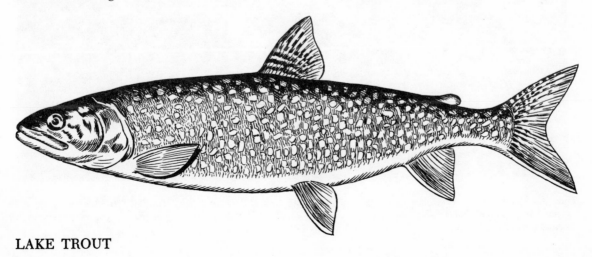

LAKE TROUT

These husky lake trout were taken in Canada where fishing is best for these fish. Most lake trout range from 5 to 15 pounds in weight but in the more remote northern areas fish up to 20 or 30 pounds are common. (CANADIAN TRAVEL BUREAU)

to 5 or 6 inches; long, large plugs, spinners with or without baits and jigs. When using a fly rod for casting or trolling you can use streamer flies such as those used for landlocked salmon.

Lake trout feed on smelt, ciscoes, tullibees, whitefish, sculpins, suckers, darters, alewives, and other minnows and small fish. These can all be used as bait or for trolling behind a spinner. They have also been caught on night crawlers and worms in some of the reservoirs in New York State.

Lake trout fishing is best early in the spring soon after the ice is out and then again in the fall when they return to the shallows to spawn. So in most areas you'll find the best fishing during April, May, early June, and then again during October and November. During the summer months when they are deep the fishing is slow. The exceptions are farther north in Canadian and Alaskan waters where the ice may not break up until June and then good fishing is often had during July and August. Lake trout are also caught through the ice during the winter months.

You can catch lake trout on any day, but many anglers prefer the windy, rainy, cloudy days.

Finding lake trout early in the spring is easy because they are usually near shore, at the mouths of inlets and streams entering into the lake and along the reefs and shoals extending from land. They prefer shoals or reefs which have deep water nearby and a bottom strewn with rocks or boulders. The smaller fish will venture into the shallows near shore but the larger ones prefer deeper water.

During the summer months locating the lake trout presents a problem since they are in very deep water then. You may find them in some lakes only 50 feet down, while in others they may be down in 100 or 200 feet of water. They like a water temperature between 40° to 45° F, so a water thermometer is a big help in finding the level where they are lying. You have to locate the submerged reefs, shoals, rocks, or holes where lake trout are congregated.

Then in the late fall you'll find them near shore again in many of the same spots where they were in the spring.

When they are in fairly shallow water near shore you can catch them by casting either from land or a boat. A boat is best because you can move around and try different spots and also cover more water by casting from different locations. Spoons and underwater plugs are best, retrieved at a slow or medium speed with plenty of action. You can try a few casts with the lure traveling just below the surface. If that doesn't produce let the lure sink deeper before you reel it back. Move the boat around and cast over a reef or shoal at different angles.

When casting doesn't produce or you want to take a rest you can try trolling. Here, too, the lures should be worked at different depths and different speeds until you find the right combination. During the summer months deep trolling must be done to reach the fish. Here you let out a wire or lead core line until you feel it hit bottom, then reel in a few feet and troll your lure at that depth. If that doesn't produce you can reel in a few more feet and troll at that depth. Once you locate the depth where the fish are, you can mark your line so that you can let out the same length every time. When using lead core, monofilament, or braided lines you need added weight such as sinkers or trolling weights to get down deep enough. These are best used with a triangle trolling rig or a three-way swivel. The sinker may range anywhere from 4 to 12 ounces depending on the depth of the water fished and the type of line being used.

Spoons and large underwater plugs are effective lures for deep trolling. But in some lakes they use a "cowbell" multiple spinner rig. This has at least four spinners rigged a few inches apart on a leader and a spoon or plug on the end. You can also use a June bug spinner and a smelt or other small fish on the hook behind it.

Lake trout can also be taken by jigging near the bottom with spoons or lead-head jigs. Here you simply let the lure down to the bottom, reel in a few inches, then work your rod up and down. A variation of this is to lower the jig to the bottom, then reel it back fast. Or you can cast it out and wait until it hits bottom, then reel back toward the surface.

When lures fail to bring a strike you can still fish with live or dead minnows or small fish. These can be lowered with a sinker to the bottom and allowed to stay there until a lake trout comes along and swallows it.

Most lake trout during the summer months are caught by deep trolling with wire lines. Note the salt-water type reels and sturdy rods used. (MINNESOTA DIVISION OF PUBLICITY)

A lake trout hooked on or near the surface on light tackle can provide an exciting battle. They run fast and even occasionally kick up a fuss on or near the surface. But a laker hooked on wire line or rigs with heavy weights or sinkers at great depths is another thing. Usually you get a disappointing fight and the fish gives up long before it reaches the surface. Of course, a big laker has plenty of weight and power and sometimes puts up a stubborn fight before being hauled up from the depths. But big lakers are rare in most waters and most of those you'll catch will go from 5 to 15 pounds. However, in parts of Canada and Alaska lake trout up to 20 or 30 pounds are common. The largest taken on rod and reel weighed 63 pounds 2 ounces and was caught in Lake Superior on May 25, 1952. But they grow much larger and lake trout of 80, 96, 102, 104, and 110 pounds have been reported caught on hand lines or in nets.

The lake trout has a fine-flavored flesh which can be fried, baked, broiled, or smoked. The Eskimos in Alaska prefer lake trout over rainbow trout when it comes to eating. In Canada lake trout appear regularly on restaurant menus. Lake trout used to be caught in large numbers in the Great Lakes commercially, but they have become scarce there due to the parasitic lamprey eel which attaches itself to the lake trout and sucks out the fish's blood and body fluids. A few recover from these attacks but many lake trout die. In recent years many studies have been made of the lamprey eel and means to wipe it out or at least control it have been sought. Great gains have been made toward this end and there is hope that lake trout will once again return to the Great Lakes in large numbers.

As stated earlier lake trout are found in many lakes in Alaska. In Canada, Saskatchewan is noted for its lake trout waters. Here you'll find them plentiful and large in Waterbury Lake, Kingsmere Lake, Lac La Ronge, Black Lake, and Lake Athabasca. In Manitoba, God's Lake is noted for its lake trout fishing. In Quebec, Lake St. John, Lake Wakonichi, Lake Mistassini, and Chibougamau Lake are some which can be fished. Of course, there are many more lakes and waters in Canada which contain lake trout. If you want information about a certain area write the Canadian Government Travel Bureau in Ottawa, Canada. In the United States, Maine has a lot of lakes which contain lake trout. In New Hampshire you'll find them in Big Greenough Pond, Silver Lake, Tarlton Lake, Squam Lake, and Newfound Lake. In Wisconsin, Green Lake is well-known for lake trout fishing. In Michigan, you can fish Torch, Elk, Crystal, and Higgins Lakes. In Idaho, they are found in Priest Lake. In Utah there is Fish Lake and Bear Lake. And in New York they can be caught in Lake George, Seneca Lake, Raquette Lake, Cayuga, Keuka, and Canandaigua Lakes. They have also been stocked in many reservoirs and lakes near New York City but fishing there is uncertain and undependable.

Chapter 12

MUSKELLUNGE

Most fresh-water anglers would like to catch a muskellunge because it is big and makes a real trophy. It also puts up a tough fight that strains the tackle and provides plenty of thrills. But not many anglers are willing to pay the price of catching a muskellunge. The musky is a moody, temperamental, unpredictable, tricky fish. It takes a lot of patience, persistence, and know-how to hook one. And it takes plenty of skill and a bit of luck to boat or land one. You may have to fish for days or even weeks before you so much as get one solid strike from a musky. Even the expert musky anglers and guides claim that it takes a week of hard fishing to catch one fish. There are many anglers who have fished for years for muskellunge and have yet to catch their first fish.

Yet there are a few anglers who have acquired reputations with their musky catches. These men and a few women, catch dozens of big muskies each season and often win contests for the biggest fish. These anglers are the musky specialists who fish only for these big fish and waste little time on other species. They usually live close to the waters they fish and concentrate on the lakes or rivers which they know contain plenty of big muskellunge. They put in many hours, days, weeks, and even months casting or trolling for muskies.

The average fresh-water angler has to confine his fishing to a weekend or a brief vacation period, usually during the poorest time of the year. This may be sufficient time to catch some trout, bass, panfish, and similar fish. But to catch a musky you'll have to allow plenty of time and make repeated trips and fish throughout the season from the spring or early summer into the late fall. To be frank, if you can't spend the time or don't have the patience to seek out a muskellunge you're better off if you confine your fishing to other species. By chance and with luck you may eventually hook a musky and with still more luck may land or boat him. In the meantime you would have had a lot of fun with smaller but more numerous and more co-operative species.

Let's take a close look at the muskellunge which most anglers know is a member of the pike family and is related to the pike and pickerel. It has the same, big, alligatorlike jaws, sharp teeth, and long body. The back is green or olive fading into gray and the belly is white.

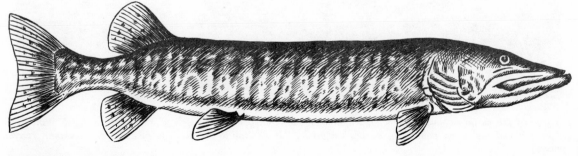

MUSKELLUNGE

A fair-sized fish as far as muskellunge go, but in some states they have to reach 30 inches to be legal. World record on rod and reel is 69 pounds 15 ounces caught by Art Lawton in the St. Lawrence River. (CANADIAN TRAVEL BUREAU)

There may be darker spots or stripes on the sides and tail, but these are often indistinct in the larger fish.

The muskellunge is known by many different names, usually different spelling versions of the more popular one. Thus you'll see them called Maskinonge, masquenonge, masquealonge, muskalonge, muskallonge, moskallonge, and similar variations. They are also called the great pike, lunge, and musky. Most anglers like to use the last name.

Muskellunge are found in the Great Lakes region north to Canada. They are also found in the St. Lawrence River and western New York and in the Ohio River and Tennessee River systems. Many waters in Wisconsin, Minnesota, and Michigan also have them. Although some fish are found as far south as North Carolina and Kentucky the musky is mostly a fish of the northern lakes and rivers.

Many muskies are hooked each season by bass or trout fishermen on light tackle but only a few of these are landed or boated. The majority of the big muskies hooked on such light tackle are lost. Yet too many anglers insist on using their regular bass or trout tackle for the king of fresh-water game fish.

If you are really interested in catching some big muskies you should get special tackle for them. A fairly stiff bait-casting rod from 5 to 6 feet long with an extra long handle is most suited for this fishing. You'll find many manufacturers making this rod and calling it a "musky" rod. With it you should use a good-quality bait-casting reel, preferably one which has a star-drag. The reel should hold at least 100 yards of braided nylon or Dacron, or monofilament line testing from 15 to 25 pounds.

You can also use spinning tackle to catch muskies but stay away from the light, limber rods used for trout or bass fishing. Get a heavy fresh-water spinning rod 6 or 7 feet long or a light salt-water spinning rod of the same weight and length. This rod should have the backbone to cast lures up to 2 ounces or so. It should be used with a large fresh-water spinning reel or one of the smaller salt-water models. You can use monofilament lines testing from 8 to 15 with such a rod. The lighter lines and rods can be used in open waters for small- and medium-sized musk-

ies. The heavier lines and rods are better for weedy waters or those with snags and rocks.

Small-sized muskies can also be taken on the heavier fly rods, but since fishing for these fresh-water tigers requires a lot of casting, the fly rod user is handicapped. You can save your wrist and arm by using a bait-casting or spinning rod. And you can cast larger and heavier lures which will interest more muskies than the smaller fly rod lures.

The rods used for muskellunge fishing are on the stiff and heavy side for several practical reasons. First, the musky has tough jaws, and in order to set the hooks you need a stiff rod. Second, you often have to use large lures to entice muskies to strike. Casting such lures requires a fairly stiff action rod. Finally, you sometimes have to turn or try to slow down a big musky heading for weeds or logs. You can do this more readily with a stiff rod and fairly strong line.

When it comes to lures used for muskies the old-time fluted spinner with feather hooks is still good for trolling. Other types of large spinners can also be cast or trolled. The wobbling spoon up to 8 inches long will take quite a few muskies. These are good in the red-and-white, silver, and chrome finishes. The spinner and big bucktail combinations account for many muskies and those with black hair seem to be very effective. Various types of surface plugs such as the poppers, swimmers, gurglers, crawlers will raise a lot of big muskellunge. Underwater plugs up to 6, 7, even 8 inches long in the solid or double-jointed models take many muskies each year.

Whichever lure you use make sure you attach a wire leader to the end of your line. Most musky fishermen who troll use wire leaders up to 3 feet long. This may be difficult to cast so you can shorten it to 8 or 10 inches.

When artificial lures fail to produce a strike you can try natural baits such as big minnows, suckers, carp, yellow perch, small pike, and walleyes. But the favored natural bait is a live or dead sucker from 8 to 12 inches long.

You may be able to catch muskies as early as March or April along their southern range if the legal season is open at that time. But farther north fishing doesn't usually start until May or June. June is a good month in most areas since the water is still cool and the fish are active and

Musky lakes are usually big and in the wilder regions such as this one in Wisconsin. The angler in the boat is casting, but trolling also takes many of these fish. (WISCONSIN CONSERVATION DEPARTMENT)

feeding. Many muskies are taken in July and August, not because they are the best months but because most anglers fish for them during the vacation season. Actually, July and August are poor months compared to later on in September and October when the biggest catches are made and the largest fish are often taken.

Muskies have been caught at almost every hour of the day, but as a general rule the best fishing is from about 9 A.M. to 3 P.M. But in some waters you'll catch them early in the morning and toward evening. And until recent years it was believed that muskies do not bite at night. But this has been disproven by some fine catches made on both dark and moonlit nights.

Most expert musky fishermen and guides agree that the best fishing usually takes place on the dark, windy, rainy days when the surface of the water is choppy or even rough.

The whole secret in musky fishing is to locate the fish first, then concentrate your efforts on making him strike. Your chances are increased if you can locate several musky hideouts and spend the day giving each one a good workout. That is why a professional guide is a big help to the beginner. He knows his waters, the habits of the fish under varying weather and water conditions. He can take you straight to the spots where he caught muskies before or knows that they are present.

If you fish without a guide you have to locate your own fish. In most waters muskies are solitary fish which take up residence in a favored location or choice feeding spot and make short forays to nearby waters, but almost always return to their home base. However, at certain times of the year and in certain waters you may run into a concentration of muskies in a relatively small area such as a cove. Then you can sometimes take several fish from that spot. However, usually a big muskie will guard his spot against all intruders, eating the smaller ones and chasing away the bigger ones. You'll catch one musky and on rare occasions two from such a spot. Then you might as well move on to another spot. But a good musky location doesn't remain empty for long. Another fish will move in soon after the original occupant is removed.

The muskies favorite hangouts in a lake include weedy, shallow areas, coves, sunken trees and brush piles, logs, rock and sand bars, points of islands, overhanging trees along shore, lily pads, and any other cover or obstruction. They also frequent the inlets and outlets to a lake where minnows, suckers, and small fish may congregate. But the preferred spots usually have a thick growth of weeds where smaller fish can hide. Muskies will lie here for hours waiting for them to come out. In rivers look for them in the larger, deeper pools, along shores with sunken trees, logs, and in the channels. If there are islands, they'll hang out along the points and drop-offs. They'll often come into very shallow water from 2 to 8 feet to feed, but return to deeper water from 10 to 25 feet during the daytime and summer months.

Another way to locate a musky is to see one feeding when it breaks water to catch a big frog, mouse, rat, muskrat, chipmunk, squirrel, duckling, gosling, or other small animal. These have all been found from time to time in their stomachs. You can also try casting a surface plug at random and watch for swirls or follow-ups behind the lure. Muskies have the exasperating habit of following lures and then refusing them near the boat. But this gives away their location and you can keep returning to the spot in the hope that on another occasion they'll grab the lure or bait.

Casting is a favorite method of catching muskellunge in lakes and rivers. This is usually done from a drifting boat moving with the wind or current. This can be done alongside weed beds, rocky bars, lily pads, and other spots where muskies are present. It is best to cast ahead of the drifting boat or well to one side. This method is best with two anglers in the boat—one handling the motor or oars and the other doing the fishing.

As a general rule it is best to retrieve the lures fairly fast for muskellunge. In fact, surface plugs are often reeled so fast that they skitter on top. However, there are other times when a medium or even slow retrieve is better. Still other times an erratic retrieve will interest the fish. But fast, medium, or slow, the lure should be lifelike and moving at all times.

Muskies will often follow a lure up to the boat, then turn around or sink without striking. Or you may get a swirl behind the lure as it travels

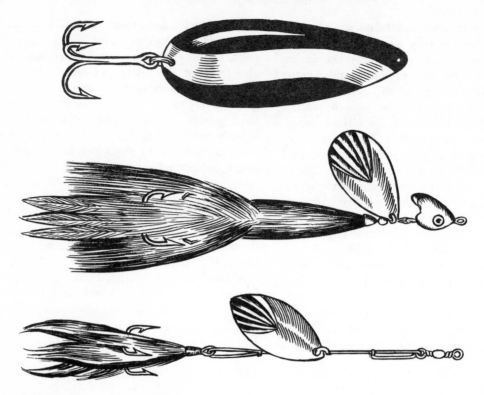

Spinner, bucktail and spoon for muskellunge

on or near the surface. When this happens speed up your retrieve and then when it gets near the boat don't take the lure out of the water. Instead, swish the lure around alongside the boat in a circle or figure-eight pattern. This will sometimes cause the musky to grab the lure right near the boat. If muskies continue to follow your lure without striking you can try changing lures to find one which may interest them.

Another popular method used for muskies is trolling with large spoons, spinners, or underwater plugs. Here you should let out anywhere from 75 to 125 feet of line and work the boat over submerged weed beds, alongside lily pads, around islands, and in channels and coves. In shallow water you don't need a weight on your line. But in deeper water where you want your lure to travel 15 or 20 feet down you may need a lead trolling weight to get the lure down.

When artificial lures don't work you can try natural baits such as a sucker. This small fish is harnessed around the head and then can be cast into likely spots. Since the sucker is dead it must be given action with the rod tip. It must be worked so that it spurts, dives, darts, and even

surfaces. You can also try letting it sink to the bottom, then retrieve it toward the surface in short jerks. Dead suckers can also be trolled slowly behind the boat. Or one can be used alive and allowed to swim around until a musky grabs it. No matter how you use suckers or other natural baits you must give the musky plenty of time to swallow them. A musky will grab the small fish in the middle, then will swim off to swallow it. You must give slack line when this happens so that the fish doesn't feel the pull on the line. Then you have to wait while the fish makes up its mind to swallow the sucker. This might take a few minutes or as long as an hour.

When you set the hook, either with lures or baits, come back hard with your rod tip. Some anglers even strike two or three times. The musky has a tough jaw and you have to penetrate it in order for the hooks to hold.

A musky puts up a spectacular fight at times, leaping, lunging, rolling, and splashing around on top of the water. Other times he sulks and makes short runs below the surface. A big musky has plenty of endurance and staying power and the fight may last a half hour or more. They will often head for sunken logs, rocks, trees, or other obstructions. Many big fish are lost near the boat when the fish makes a last, sudden surge or thrashes around on top.

A musky should be played until it gives up—and turns over on its side. Then you can use a wide-mouthed net to scoop up the smaller fish. If the fish is large it is better to gaff it through the lower lip or jaw. Some expert anglers and guides grab the musky in the eye sockets or under the gill covers. A big musky can also be beached on a sloping shore if the angler gets out of the boat in shallow water.

It is believed that muskies reach over 100 pounds in weight, but the largest taken on rod and reel weighed 69 pounds 15 ounces. This was caught in New York State by Art Lawton on September 22, 1957, in the St. Lawrence River. Through the years many other muskies in the 40-, 50-, and 60-pound classes have been caught. But in most waters you're lucky to catch a musky in the 15- to 30-pound class. Some outstanding musky catches on light tackle have been made by Len Hartman of Ogdensburg, New York. He uses spinning tackle and holds many records for muskies on light lines. His biggest fish was a 67-pound 15-ounce musky caught in the St. Lawrence River on 11-lb test line.

Some of the best muskellunge waters are found in Canada, particularly Ontario, where the Lake of the Woods, Vermilion Lake, and Eagle Lake are famous. In the United States there are more than five hundred lakes in Wisconsin where muskies are found. Some of the most productive are Chippewa Flowage, Wisconsin River, Eagle River and Eagle Lake, Pelican Lake, Lac Vieux Desert, Grindstone Lake, Flambeau River, Hayward Lake, Lac Court Oreilles, and Big Arbor Vitae Lake. In Michigan, Lake St. Clair, Gun Lake, Thunder Bay, Munusconong Bay, Tahquamenon River, and Detroit River are also noted for musky fishing. In Minnesota, Leech Lake has produced many fish of good size. In New York, Chautauqua Lake, the St. Lawrence River, and the Finger Lakes chain are fished. In West Virginia, the Little Kanawha River, Elk River, Big Coal River, Mill Creek, West Fork, Middle Island Creek, and Salt Lick Creek contain muskies. Muskellunge are also found in some waters in Indiana, Ohio, Vermont, Pennsylvania, North Carolina, Kentucky, and Tennessee.

But no matter where you seek them muskies offer a challenge and require plenty of skill and know-how to catch them. If you catch a good-sized musky you can feel proud because you have accomplished one of the more difficult feats in fresh-water fishing.

Chapter 13

PIKE

At one time very few anglers, in this country or in Canada, fished for pike deliberately. In the early days there was such an abundance of trout, bass, salmon, and other fresh-water fish that the pike was overlooked or scorned in favor of these supposedly more desirable fishes. Today, there are still a few die-hards who consider the pike unworthy of the title of "game fish" and prefer other species. And in Canada and Alaska, where pike are very plentiful together with other game fish, they are still hated or ignored by the natives in those areas.

Many anglers who despise the pike point to its destructiveness of other fish and young waterfowl. They claim that many good trout and bass waters have been ruined by the introduction of pike. These greedy fish are supposed to have eaten up most of the trout and bass in those waters. In Canada pike devour hundreds of thousands if not millions of ducklings in Saskatchewan and Manitoba.

But a look at the other side of the picture shows that in many waters trout, bass, walleyes, and pike have lived together for ages and each species is plentiful. Pike may be detrimental to certain waters where trout and bass may decline in numbers when pike first appear. But in many other waters biologists claim that pike actually improve the fishing by keeping down the numbers of yellow perch, sunfish, and other panfish. True, they'll also eat trout and bass, but the fish that are left grow larger in size in lakes or rivers where pike are present. In waters where pike are absent, panfish and bass become plentiful but stunted in size.

But whether you admire the pike or hate him, you are missing some good fishing if you don't try to catch the slim, toothy predators. Except for coloring the pike looks like a smaller replica of his close relative—the muskellunge. However, pike are more numerous and are found in more waters than the musky. They are also less tem-

PIKE

A weedy shoreline is a favorite hangout of the pike. (NEBRASKA GAME COMMISSION)

peramental and not so fussy about taking a lure or bait as the musky.

The pike has been called the great northern pike, northern pike, jackfish, jack, grass pike, and snake. The term "pickerel" is also used in some areas but this, of course, confuses it with the true pickerels.

The pike has a long body with the dorsal fin set way back near the tail. The mouth looks like a big duck's bill or alligator's snout. Most pike are olive or greenish in color with an occasional bluish cast. The color becomes lighter toward the belly which is yellowish or white. There are many yellow-white bean-shaped spots along the sides of the body. However, there is also a so-called "silver pike" which is bluish gray in color which lacks the lighter spots. This variant is found in some waters in Minnesota and Wisconsin.

The pike is one of the most widely distributed fish to be found in the United States, Canada, Alaska, Europe, and Asia. Although in this country the pike has been introduced into many waters and as far south as North Carolina, it is mainly a fish of the colder, northern waters.

For small pike you can use your regular bass or walleye fishing tackle such as a light or medium bait-casting rod, spinning rod or fly rod. For larger northerns the same tackle used for muskellunge (see preceding chapter on muskellunge) will be the most practical. This is especially true when fishing around weeds, rocks, logs, or other obstructions. A good all-around outfit is a spinning or spin-casting rod of medium or heavy weight, a spinning or spin-casting reel to match filled with lines testing from 10 to 20 pounds. The lighter lines are best for light lures, small fish, and open waters. The heavier lines can be used for heavy lures, big fish, and snag-filled waters.

For the utmost in thrills you can use a fly rod, fly reel, and weight-forward fly line. The type of rod used for black bass, steelhead, or Atlantic salmon is fine. Streamer and bucktail flies are the best lures to use with a fly rod, although at times the popping bass bugs or minnow type bugs also work when pike are hitting on the surface.

Lures used with casting rods or spinning rods include surface plugs, underwater plugs, and spoons in silver, chrome, nickel, copper, red-and-white and black-and-white finishes. Large spinners with feathers or bucktail are used mostly for trolling. Another good trolling lure is a June-bug spinner with a minnow hooked on a tandem hook.

Pike will also take various natural baits such as frogs, minnows, chubs, suckers, yellow perch, whitefish, and other small fish.

When using either artificial lures or natural baits it is important to have a wire leader at least 8 or 10 inches long attached to the end of the line. For trolling it can even be longer. Pike, like muskies, have sharp teeth which will often sever an ordinary fishing line or nylon leader.

The top months for catching pike in most waters are May, June, September, and October. The early spring is a good time because the pike are in shallow water for spawning purposes. Small pike are often taken during the summer months, but the larger pike bite best in the fall after Labor Day. If you want to catch good-sized pike during July and August your best bet is one of the lakes or rivers in the northern sections of Canada. Here the water is still cold and the fish are numerous and hungry.

Most pike are caught during the daytime and only a small number are occasionally taken at night. In the spring and late fall pike are found near shore much of the day. But during the summer months they seek deeper water during the middle of the day. They may come into the shallow water in the summer in the early morning or evening. Most pike anglers like to fish on the windy, stormy, cloudy days when they claim these fish are more active and more likely to hit.

When feeding or hiding, pike love to lie in or near weed beds, around stumps, lily pads, sunken trees, logs, and other cover. In lakes look for them around the shallow portions, in coves, weeds, reefs, points of land, exposed and submerged sand or gravel bars, inlets and outlets to the lake. In rivers they are more common in the deeper pools, quieter backwaters, below obstructions such as dams, falls, log jams, rocks, and boulders. As a general rule, pike are found in water from 2 to 12 feet deep in the spring and fall and when feeding early in the morning or evening in the summer. When they are resting,

This 27½-pound pike is one of the largest ever caught on rod and reel in Nebraska. (NEBRASKA GAME COMMISSION)

or during the hot summer months, they may lie in deeper water. Big pike, especially, like to stay near a deep hole or drop-off between feeding periods.

Like big muskies, big pike are often solitary and take up locations which they hold against smaller fish. But smaller pike are often found in fairly heavy concentrations and several fish can often be taken from a comparatively small area. Even big pike tend to congregate in large numbers in a certain cove or pool in the wilderness lakes and rivers in Canada. As many as fifty or more pike have been caught from a single cove or bay in such waters.

It is often easy to catch pike in wilderness waters where they are plentiful and unsophisticated. But in the more heavily fished lakes near the larger population centers pike soon learn to avoid most lures and baits. Then you have to know how to work your lures to get strikes and put in plenty of time casting for the fish. One of the best methods is to cast an underwater plug or spoon from an anchored or drifting boat outside weed beds or other pike hangouts. Different depths and speeds of retrieve should be tried until you find the right combination. Sometimes a steady retrieve will work, while other times an erratic one will be better.

Pike have the same habit as the musky in that they will often follow a lure right up to the boat without striking. When this happens, try speeding up the lure and if the fish comes right up to the boat keep the lure in the water, swishing it around in circles or figure eights. Sometimes the pike will grab the lure alongside the boat if you do this.

Another way to catch pike is to troll for them over sunken weed beds, alongside lily pads, along the edges of sand or rock bars and other pike spots. A favorite trolling lure is a spinner and feathers or a spinner such as the June bug with a minnow. Spoons and underwater plugs can also be used for trolling. Best results are usually obtained by moving slowly but with enough speed to bring out the action in the lure.

A pike usually smashes a lure hard and often hooks itself, but it's a good idea to set the hook with the rod to make sure. A big pike like his musky brother has tough jaws and large or dull hooks require force to set them properly.

During the summer months pike can be caught by still fishing with live baits such as frogs, minnows, suckers, and other small fish. A fairly large frog can be used with a frog harness and can be cast around weeds or lily pads. Minnows and suckers from 4 to 10 inches in length make a good bait and can be hooked through the back. If fishing over a sunken weed bed you can add a cork or plastic float or bobber on the line to keep the bait a foot or so away from the tops of the weeds. A pike usually grabs the minnow or sucker in the middle, then makes a short run after which he stops to swallow the bait. When he starts moving once more is the time to strike to set the hook.

On light tackle pike will put up a good fight, with the smaller ones up to 10 or 12 pounds often jumping out of the water. These smaller fish are also faster and more active. Larger pike are slower and do most of their battling below the surface. Pike also have the habit of allowing themselves to be led up to the boat without much fuss—then suddenly go into a frenzy, leaping or thrashing around on top, or making a run. This will often take the angler by surprise and the sudden strain may break the line or straighten a hook.

Pike should be played until they give up completely and turn over on their sides before an attempt is made to land them. A large, wide-mouthed net can be used for the smaller fish. The larger fish can be gaffed through the lower lip. Experienced anglers and guides sometimes grab the pike in the gills or by placing a thumb and forefinger into the eye sockets.

It's also a good idea to have a billy or club handy so you can bop the pike on the head to stun him and stop him from thrashing around. A pair of long-nosed pliers are also good for removing the hooks from the pike's mouth.

Pike can also be caught during the winter months through the ice in states where this is legal. Here you use a tip-up and a live minnow for bait. The minnow is lowered through the hole in the ice until it is almost near the bottom or a foot or two above the submerged weeds.

The world record pike caught on rod and reel is a 46-pound 2-ounce fish caught in the Sacandaga Reservoir, New York, by Peter Dubuc on September 15, 1940. In Canada pike from 20 to

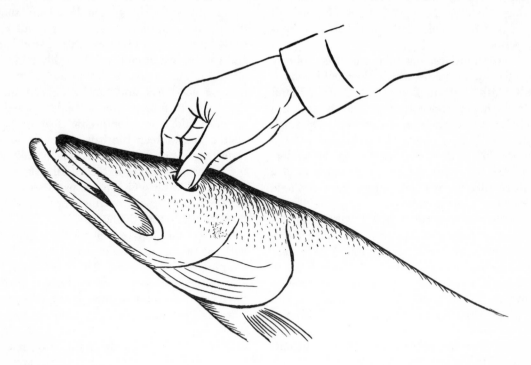

Grabbing pike in eyesockets

30 pounds are often taken. The largest pike have been reported from European waters and they are believed to grow up to 60 or perhaps 70 pounds.

Although pike are somewhat bony they make good eating if you fillet the smaller ones and fry them. They can also be baked and smoked.

The best pike fishing is found in Canada especially in Manitoba, Saskatchewan, and Ontario. In Ontario, Lac Seul and the Nipigon River are favored. In Saskatchewan, Athabaska Lake, Reindeer Lake, and Cree Lake have some big pike. In Manitoba, God's Lake, Reed Lake, Flin Flon, Cranberry Portage, and the Pas are great pike waters. Of course, there are hundreds of other lakes and rivers in Canada which contain pike. In the United States you'll find pike in Alaska, Nebraska, Iowa, Missouri, Minnesota, Wisconsin, Michigan, New York, and the New England states.

Chapter 14

PICKEREL

On the days when black bass aren't hitting, many anglers in our Eastern states settle for pickerel. This smallest member of the pike family fills a niche somewhere between the black bass and the panfishes. He's not quite as desirable as the black bass yet he's bigger and more of a true game fish than most of the panfishes. But to a surprising number of anglers the pickerel is more than just merely a fill-in fish. Thousands of anglers go fishing for pickerel deliberately both during the summer and winter months. In New Jersey, when a vote was taken on the most popular fish in the state, the pickerel came out ahead. There he's popular with still fishermen, fly fishermen and, spin and baitcasters.

Another reason why the pickerel is popular is due to the fact that this fish is able to withstand a wide spread of water temperatures. He's found in warm, sluggish ponds and streams and in the colder lakes and rivers. So if you live in one of the Eastern states you'll probably find a pickerel pond, lake, or river nearby. And he's a willing striker—almost always ready to hit a lure or take a bait.

There are actually three species of pickerels found in the United States: the chain pickerel, the redfin or barred pickerel, and the grass or mud pickerel. As far as anglers are concerned the chain pickerel is the only worthwhile species because the redfin and grass pickerels rarely grow over 12 inches in length.

The chain pickerel has many names such as the banded pickerel, common pickerel, eastern pickerel, reticulated pickerel, eastern pike, grass pike, green pike, chain pike, jack, jackfish, and snake.

Once you've seen a few pickerel you can't mistake them for young muskies or pike. They have dark green or brownish green backs shading into a lighter green and yellow on the sides. The belly is white and the chainlike dark markings cover the sides of the fish from the gill cover to the tail.

The pickerel is found in Canada in Nova Scotia, New Brunswick, and southeastern Quebec. In the United States his range is from Maine south to Florida and Alabama and west to the Mississippi Valley, Texas, Missouri, and the Tennessee River system. However, they

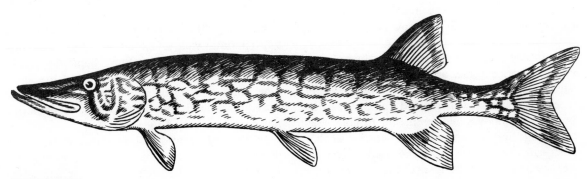

PICKEREL

Many pickerel are caught during the winter months through the ice on our northern lakes. Live minnows are the preferred bait but pickerel may hit a spoon or jig worked up and down. (PHOTO BY JOHNNY NICKLAS, PENNSYLVANIA FISH COMMISSION)

have been introduced widely and are found in many waters.

Pickerel can be caught with cane poles, fly rods, bait-casting, and spinning rods. The most popular nowadays is a light-spinning or spincasting rod with 4- or 6-pound test line. But the cane pole is still used by many for still fishing with bait or for skittering.

In fishing lures the small spoons in red-and-white, silver, chrome, and brass or copper finishes are good. So are the various types of weighted spinners. Unweighted spinners can be used with minnows, and worms for trolling. Surface plugs and underwater plugs in the smaller sizes can also be used. Fly rod anglers can try surface bass bugs or poppers of the minnow type and streamer and bucktail flies.

In the natural baits the top bait is a minnow from 2½ to 3½ inches long. This can be a shiner or chub and in the coastal areas the saltwater killifish often makes a good bait. Pickerel will also take night crawlers, crayfish, and frogs at times.

Pickerel will start biting early in the year and will continue well into the fall. The top months are usually April, May, June, September, and October. They can be caught during the summer months too in many waters. Winter fishing through the ice is excellent in many lakes in our northern and New England states.

In the spring and fall you can often catch pickerel throughout the day. But during the summer months the early morning or late afternoon and evening are best. However, if the day

This is considered a pretty big pickerel—most of them are smaller and thinner. This happy angler caught this one in Peck's Pond, Pennsylvania. (PHOTO BY JOHNNY NICKLAS, PENNSYLVANIA FISH COMMISSION)

is cloudy, rainy, or stormy you can often have good fishing during the middle of the day even in the summer.

Pickerel usually prefer the shallow areas and quieter waters and the weedy areas of lakes and rivers. When feeding they are often found close to shore in weed beds, coves, under lily pads and around logs, rocks, sunken trees, and other obstructions. In rivers you'll find them more in the quieter, slower pools, eddies, backwaters, and coves. They will often come into extremely shallow water a few inches deep with their dorsal fins protruding above the surface.

Although thousands of pickerel are caught still fishing with cane poles you can have more fun if you use a light spinning rod or fly rod. The minnow should be hooked through the lips or back and a light float or bobber should be attached about 3 or 4 feet above the bait. This can be cast into likely looking spots and allowed to remain there for a few minutes. Or you can fish in a moving boat drifting with the wind or current and let your minnow swim behind the boat about 20 or 30 feet away. In still fishing it is important to give the pickerel plenty of time to swallow the bait. They usually grab the minnow crosswise in their mouths, swim away a short distance and then stop to swallow it. When they start moving once more set the hook.

Casting lures such as small spoons, spinners, surface and underwater plugs can be very effective especially early in the morning and evening. Such lures should be retrieved slowly but with plenty of action such as short, quick jerks and stop-and-go movements. And work all the lures right up to the boat or shore. Pickerel will often follow the lure for a long distance and then suddenly decide to strike just as the lure leaves the water.

When casting, try all the shallow water near shore, next to weeds, lily pads, and rocks or logs. If a pickerel is seen in shallow water don't get too close but make a long cast well beyond the fish and reel in the lure a few feet ahead of him. They are very skittish in shallow water and a big commotion, disturbance, or sight of a man will frighten them.

Fly rod anglers can have a lot of fun using streamers or bucktails or minnow-type bass bugs. These should be worked close to the shore in shallow water and should imitate a crippled or frightened minnow.

Trolling also accounts for many pickerel and is a good way to take the fish during the summer months when they are in deeper water. A spoon or spinner and minnow combination are two good lures for trolling.

Skittering was a popular and effective way to take pickerel years ago. It is still used by some anglers and is a deadly method if practiced correctly. A long cane or glass pole about 14 or 16 feet long is used and on the end of the line a minnow, frog, strip of pork rind, or the belly and two fins of a yellow perch or sunfish is impaled on a hook. This is skittered or jerked along the surface in short spurts. It is most effective in the open pockets among lily pads, weed beds, and around stumps and logs.

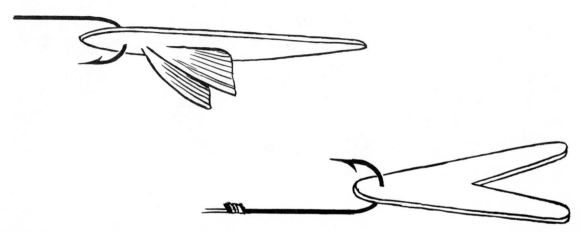

Perch belly and pork rind used in skittering

Winter fishing through the ice is popular with many fishermen, and on many lakes and ponds accounts for more and bigger pickerel than are taken during the summer months. Here you can use a small, live minnow such as a shiner and lower it close to the bottom.

A pickerel on the end of a line will put up a good fight if given a chance on light tackle. Sometimes he'll come in with little resistance, but usually when he sees the boat he'll suddenly break loose with a series of wild leaps, twists, and surface acrobatics which will surprise and delight the angler. He hasn't got much endurance, however, and soon quits and can be netted. The hook tears out of his tender mouth easily so don't horse him or try to lift him out of the water.

Most of the chain pickerel caught will run from 1 to 3 pounds in weight. In some waters they may reach 5 or 6 pounds, but such fish are rare. A 9-pound 3-ounce pickerel was caught on July 6, 1957, by Frank McGovern in Aetna Lake, New Jersey. A few other pickerel going 9 pounds or a few ounces more have been caught through the ice.

Pickerel have a sweet, white, tasty meat but they are somewhat bony. They should be cleaned and scaled soon after being caught. The big ones can be baked or cut into steaks or fillets and fried. Smaller ones can be split open and fried.

If you live in one of the states where pickerel are found you'll probably know of or locate waters containing these fish near your home. They are especially plentiful in New England, New York, New Jersey, Pennsylvania, Delaware, and Maryland.

Chapter 15

WALLEYE

In many of our northern states the walleye is sought by more anglers than any other species. It is especially popular with many anglers because it reaches a good size and makes delicious eating. Also, it is often easier to catch than trout, bass, pike, or muskies. But don't get the idea that walleye fishing is simple and all you have to do is drop your bait in the water or cast out your lure and reel it back. Walleyes are often difficult to locate at certain times of the year. And you have to present the bait at the right level and give it the right action to get strikes.

Walleyes are known by many names such as pike perch, yellow pike, jack salmon, golden pike, yellow pickerel, Susquehanna salmon, opal eye, pickerel, and dore. The last two names are used in Canada. There is also a subspecies of walleye known as the blue pike, blue walleye, and blue pickerel.

The walleye varies in color depending on where it is found, but is usually a dark olive or brassy color mottled with yellow. The fins may be yellowish or pinkish. There is a dark spot at the rear of the front dorsal fin. The walleye has a large mouth and strong canine teeth. The eye is large, whitish, and glassy.

Walleyes are found from Canada southward and eastward to North Carolina, Georgia, Alabama, Arkansas, and Tennessee. They are plentiful throughout the Great Lakes region.

You don't need any special tackle to catch walleyes. You can use almost any bait-casting, spinning or spin-casting outfit you have. Light tackle will provide the most sport, and only when fishing in certain areas and for extremely big walleyes do you need somewhat heavier tackle. Fly rods can be used in certain waters when the fish are in shallow water near shore.

The most effective lure for walleyes is usually a spinner such as the June-bug type with a double hook behind it covered with a minnow, worms, or lamprey eel. They will also take various types of spoons and weighted spinners. Deep-running and sinking underwater plugs are also good at times. And in recent years some fine catches have been made on the lead-head jigs.

Although natural baits are often used with spinners they will also take walleyes when still fished. A lively minnow or small fish on a hook will often catch them. Another good bait is a soft-shelled crayfish.

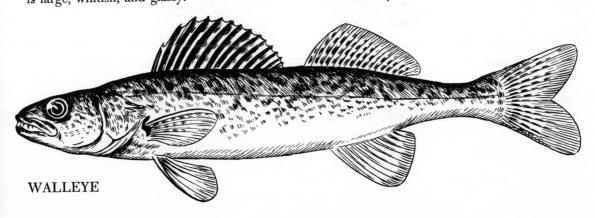

WALLEYE

Walleyes are great cold-weather fish and are often caught in the early spring, late fall, and during the winter months. This is a hefty 10-pound fish being netted from Wallenpaupack Creek, Pennsylvania. (PHOTO BY JOHNNY NICKLAS, PENNSYLVANIA FISH COMMISSION)

The walleye is a cold-water fish which is most active during the spring, fall, and winter months. In southern waters such as Kentucky and Tennessee the fish move up the rivers to spawn as early as February and good fishing is experienced then and into March. Farther north, the spawning run takes place in April and May. Good fishing is generally experienced during May, June, September, October, and November. They can be caught during the summer months but the fishing is better farther north in Canada at this time.

In the spring and late fall you can often catch walleyes most of the day. But during the summer months the early morning, late afternoon, and evening and night hours are best. In fact, walleyes do a lot of feeding at night from spring to fall and you stand a good chance of catching them in the dark. During the summer months if you must fish during the day choose the cloudy, rainy days. Or fish early in the morning, at dusk, and during the night.

Locating walleyes may be simple or very difficult depending on the area, season, and time of day. Walleyes are also great wanderers moving about in schools to different sections of a lake or river. In the spring when the walleyes move up rivers to spawn they are more concentrated in smaller areas and are easier to locate. They also feed closer to shore and in shallow water during the spring and late fall months.

In rivers, look for walleyes below dams, falls, rapids, or riffles, around rocks, boulders, and in the quieter pools and eddies. Toward evening they may move into shallow water around rock ledges, sand bars, shoals, and points of land. Look for concentrations of minnows in the late afternoon and evening in shallow water or coves. Walleyes often come in to feed on them and great sport can be had.

In lakes, fish around rocky points, rock or gravel bars, weedy bays and deep water bordering rocky shores. The mouths of streams or rivers entering a lake are also good locations.

As a general rule fish the shallow inshore waters early in the morning, in the evening and at night. Fish the deeper waters in the middle of the day. Walleyes are usually found in water from 3 to 30 feet deep, but in some lakes they may go down to 50 or 60 feet during the summer months.

A good way to locate walleyes is by slow trolling. Of course, you can also catch them by trolling with a June-bug spinner and a minnow or worms on the hook. Lamprey eels are very good on a hook also in rivers where this bait is found. Trolling is done slowly by bumping and feeling bottom with the sinker of the trolling rig to make sure that the lure is down deep enough. You can use the walleye rig illustrated here for this trolling. The line from the three-way swivel to the sinker can be weaker than the leader holding the lure or the main fishing line. Then if the sinker gets snagged it can be broken off saving the rest of the rig.

Somewhat similar to trolling is drifting for walleyes with the wind across a lake. This is especially effective over wide areas such as sunken weed beds, gravel bars, sand bars, and reefs. You can use the same rig as for trolling for this and such baits as minnows, small fish, and spinners and worms.

Once you locate a school of walleyes by trolling or drifting drop anchor and cast to them. Lures such as underwater plugs, weighted spinners, spoons, and jigs are best for this and they should be allowed to sink deep. The retrieve should be slow, but fast enough to bring out the action of the lure. In a river, a jig is one of the best lures for getting down into the pockets or holes where walleyes are lying. The jig may have to be cast upstream and across to get down deep enough and then is allowed to swing from the fast current into the slower spots. The strike usually comes as the jig reaches the hole or pocket where the walleye is waiting.

Many walleyes are also caught by still fishing with live minnows. In fast rivers you can use the walleye rig illustrated with a somewhat shorter leader when casting is done. The rig is baited with a minnow and is cast into the river and allowed to drift down with the current. When it hits bottom let it rest for a few minutes, then lift the rod tip and let it drift to a new spot farther downstream. Then let it rest again in the new location. By doing this you cover more area and keep the bait moving.

In a lake, fishing from a boat you can often dispense with the sinker if using minnows which head down toward the bottom. But if the minnow is the kind which stays up high near the surface, a light sinker can be used to take it

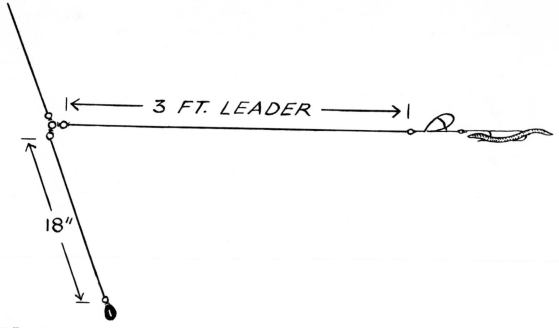

Walleye rig

down to the bottom. The minnow should be raised up and down every so often to prevent it from hiding in the weeds.

When a walleye grabs the bait give him plenty of time to swallow it before you set the hook. Walleyes usually take a bait slowly and chomp on it, trying to get it down their throats. Some anglers even give the fish slack line to make it easier to do this and avoid pulling the bait out of the fish's mouth.

Once you hook a walleye on a lure or bait, you'll have some sport and action but don't expect the speed and flash of a trout or bass. Walleyes don't jump, don't make long or fast runs nor do they have much endurance. But a good-sized fish on light tackle can provide some fun especially if hooked in a fast-moving river.

A wide-mouthed net is best for boating a big walleye. Watch out for their sharp teeth when removing lures or hooks from their mouths.

Most of the walleyes that are caught will average from 2 to 8 pounds and any fish over that size is a big one. However, in some areas and during certain seasons, big walleyes are commonly taken. Such as the spawning runs in the Cumberland River, Kentucky, when fish from 8 to 15 pounds are caught in large numbers. They've been caught up to 25 pounds in this

area, but the official rod and reel record for many years has been a 22-pound 4-ounce walleye caught by Patrick E. Noon. This was taken at Fort Erie, Ontario, on May 26, 1943.

No matter what their size, most anglers agree that the walleye is one of the best fish for the table to be caught in fresh water. They have a firm, sweet, tasty flesh which can be fried, baked, broiled, or boiled.

The walleye is widely distributed in North America but some spots are more outstanding than others for the size or number of fish caught. You can't beat Canada where they are distributed from Lake Athabaska across Alberta and Saskatchewan, down into the Hudson Bay basin, throughout the Great Lakes drainage basin and over into Labrador, Quebec, and Ontario.

In the United States, they are especially plentiful in Wisconsin where such waters as Lake Winnebago, Red Cedar River, Wapogasset Lake, Balsam Lake, Half Moon Lake, Yellow River, St. Croix Lake, Eau Claire Lakes, Whitefish Lake, and Lac Court Oreilles are fished. In Minnesota they are stocked in over 800 lakes with Fish Hook Lake, Mille Lacs, and the Red Lakes outstanding waters for them. In Michigan, the Menominee, Michigan, and Muskegon Rivers are good as are Gratiot Lake, Lake Bellaire, and

Fillets from large walleyes like these make mouth-watering meals. Raymond Suk caught these six and seven pound beauties from a reservoir. (PHOTO BY JOHNNY NICKLAS, PENNSYLVANIA FISH COMMISSION)

Hubbard Lake. In Illinois, the Mississippi River and Kankakee River contain walleyes. In Pennsylvania, the Susquehanna and Delaware Rivers are noted for walleyes. In New York, the St. Lawrence River, Lake Champlain, and the Delaware River have produced many walleyes. In New Jersey, the Delaware is also fished for walleyes. In Tennessee, Center Hill Lake, Dale Hollow Lake, and the Tennessee River are popular walleye waters. And in Kentucky, Lake Cumberland, the Cumberland River, Rockcastle River, and Laurel River have great runs of walleyes.

Naturally, there are many other states and waters which provide walleye fishing. Write to your state fish and game department for a list of lakes or rivers containing walleyes in your area.

Chapter 16

YELLOW PERCH

The yellow perch, next to the sunfishes, is one of the most popular panfish to be found in the United States. It lives in many ponds, lakes, and large, slow-moving rivers, and may even descend to brackish water when found in coastal rivers. It is usually abundant in most waters and is found in large schools and is a willing biter. All this makes the yellow perch popular with many fresh-water anglers. You'll be convinced if you ever go to the Great Lakes region in the early spring and see the thousands of yellow perch fishermen gathered there. Anglers of all ages and both sexes line the shore, bridges, piers, and small creeks and all of them are busy pulling in yellow perch.

Yellow perch are found in the Hudson Bay drainage of eastern Canada south to Kansas and northern Missouri, Illinois, Indiana, and Pennsylvania. Along the Atlantic Coast they are found from Nova Scotia to the Carolinas. They have also been introduced into California, Washington, and many other areas.

The yellow perch has been called the red perch, raccoon perch, ringed perch, zebra perch, lake perch, striped perch, and convict. It is easily identified by its six to eight broad dark stripes over a yellow body. The back is an olive or drab green color. The ventral and anal fins are a reddish orange.

You can catch yellow perch on most of the tackle used for other panfish such as the cane or glass pole, spinning rod and reel, bait-casting rod and reel and fly rod. The cane pole is best when the perch are in shallow water near shore

YELLOW PERCH

This angler knows the yellow perch is one of our best eating fish and he's icing down his catch. Perch run in the spring in irrigation ditches and small streams tributary to the Great Lakes. (MICHIGAN DEPARTMENT OF CONSERVATION)

or when fishing from boats. The fly rod, too, is used mostly for shore fishing in shallow water or from boats. For deep-water casting or still fishing a spinning rod and reel or bait-casting outfit is more practical. Both the spinning and bait-casting outfits can also be used for trolling for the perch.

If you plan to use artificial lures for yellow perch with a fly rod you'll find wet flies such as the Silver Doctor, Yellow Sally, Parmachene Belle in sizes No. 10 or 12 good. But they'll take almost any trout pattern at times. Small streamer flies in red, yellow, or white color combinations are also effective for yellow perch.

For casting with a light bait-casting rod or spinning rod or spin-casting rod, the weighted spinners, spinner and worm combinations, spinner and fly combinations, and tiny spoons and plugs are used.

However, most anglers seeking yellow perch use natural baits and among these the live minnow is tops. Small minnows, no bigger than 2 inches in length are best and these should be used on small No. 6 or 8 hooks. Millions of perch have also been caught on worms and the smaller garden worms are better than the larger angleworms. Other baits include the tail of a small crayfish, beetles, grasshoppers, crickets, grubs, and leeches. When found near salt-water yellow perch can also be caught on the small grass shrimp which live in bays and tidal creeks. Two or three of these on a hook are offered to the fish.

The yellow perch is one of the first fish to bite early in the spring. They run up the rivers and creeks and into shallow bays to spawn around April and May and many are caught at this time. But they are often caught throughout the year from spring to late fall and in the winter months they are often taken through the ice.

There is no special time of the day to go yellow perch fishing. You'll catch them all day long in the spring and fall. During the summer months when they are in deeper water the fishing may be better early in the morning and in the evening. As a rule, they are not caught too often at night.

During the spawning season, yellow perch are often easy to locate since they come in close to shore into shallow bays or run up rivers and streams. Later on, when they have finished spawning they may spread out more and wander about in schools of varying sizes. In rivers they are found in the larger, quieter pools, below dams, around old piers, sunken trees, under bridges, and near pilings and stumps. In lakes they are found in the coves and bays, channels, and along the drop-offs. Sometimes you can see them in the morning or late afternoon near the surface in large schools.

During the hot summer months a few small yellow perch may be caught near shore during the day. But most of the larger ones go into deeper water from 20 to 50 feet deep. In very deep lakes they may be down as far as 80 feet. Then in the late fall they once again return to the shallow bays, coves, harbors, canals, and mouths of streams.

One good way to locate yellow perch is to drift with the wind in a boat slowly towing a hook baited with a minnow or worm. Or you can troll slowly by rowing with a spinner and fly. When you get a perch you can drop the anchor and fish all around the boat.

Still fishing is the most popular way to catch yellow perch. A light, sensitive float or bobber is attached to the line and the baited hook should hang below it so that it almost reaches the bottom or the top of the weeds. The bait should be lively to attract the perch. It also helps if you keep moving the bait slowly back and forth to catch the attention of the fish. The yellow perch is a great bait-stealer, so don't give him too much time when you get the first nibbles. Wait a few seconds and then set the hook.

When using artificial lures such as spinners or spoons cast to the edges of weed beds or lily pads and retrieve slowly. When they are down deep let the lure sink almost to the bottom and then reel in as slowly as possible. The same thing can be done with wet flies but there you can add a split-shot or two to the leader. Sometimes a piece of worm or tiny sliver of pork rind can be added to the fly or lure to obtain more strikes. The main thing to remember when using lures is that yellow perch are slow, lazy, and cannot catch a fast-moving lure. So work the lure as slowly as you can with short jerks, twitches, and alternate pauses to give the perch time to catch and grab it.

The yellow perch is often caught during the

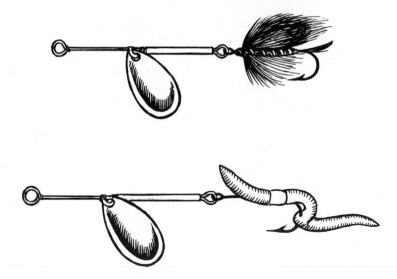

Spinners with fly and worm for yellow perch

winter months through the ice by the hardy ice fishermen. On Lake Mendota in Wisconsin many fisherman catch fifty, a hundred, two hundred or more yellow perch in a single day. For ice fishing a short rod or stick from 30 to 40 inches long can be used. The line can be a monofilament about 20 or 30 pounds for easy handling. You can also use a line on a spool with a tip-up. To the end of the lines you attach a hook and bait it with a small live minnow from 1½ to 2 inches long. Goldenrod grubs found in the boils on goldenrod stalks also make good bait. Still other baits include corn borers, salmon eggs, and an eye from the perch itself. Or you can try one of the ice flies, tiny jigs or spoons and jig with these up and down near the bottom.

Some days the fish will be in the shallows where the water is only from 8 to 15 feet deep. Other days you'll have better fishing in water 50 to 60 feet deep. Usually the peak periods are early in the morning and in the evening. Watch where other anglers fish or have chopped holes in the ice and fish near them.

The yellow perch is not much of a fighter on the end of a line. He pulls feebly and gives up too

quickly compared to other panfish and game fish. The big ones reaching 2 or 3 pounds may provide some fun on ultralight spinning tackle or a fly rod. But unfortunately, in many lakes perch are on the small side rarely going over a pound in weight. In some waters they are so numerous that they never reach more than a few inches in length and a fraction of a pound in weight. The largest yellow perch caught on rod and reel weighed 4 pounds 3½ ounces and was caught at Bordentown, New Jersey, in May 1865 by Dr. C. C. Abbot.

Even though yellow perch fight poorly many anglers will spend hours fishing for them because of their eating qualities. The yellow perch is one of the tastiest fish found in fresh water with a white, sweet, flaky meat. They are tough to scale, however, so keep them wet and clean them as soon as possible.

If you live near the Great Lakes you can go fishing for yellow perch in Lake Michigan, Lake Erie, Lake Ontario, and Lake Huron. They are also plentiful in most of the New England and Middle Atlantic states.

Ice fishing for yellow perch is a popular sport with winter anglers. They can be caught on live minnows or by jigging with small spoons and jigs. (PHOTO BY JOHNNY NICKLAS, PENNSYLVANIA FISH COMMISSION)

Chapter 17

BLUEGILL

Almost every farm kid or country boy has fished for sunfish and has a warm spot in his heart for these small, but colorful fishes. Even in later years many an older angler turns to sunfish for a day's sport and fine eating afterward. For the sunfishes are obliging little critters, almost always willing to bite. Many a fishing trip is saved for the fresh-water angler when he can't catch other fish and must turn to the sunfishes to salvage the day and bolster his ego. And sunfish are found in most rivers, lakes, ponds, and creeks near home. The result is that millions of anglers fish for them and more sunfish are probably caught than the so-called game fishes.

The sunfish family is a large one including the black basses, crappies, warmouth, rock bass, and the various species of sunfish. They are the bluegill, pumpkinseed, redbreast sunfish, redear sunfish, longear sunfish, green sunfish, and spotted sunfish. Most of the information here concerns the bluegill sunfish which is the largest and the most popular. But it can be used to catch the other kinds of sunfish too.

The bluegill sunfish is called bream, pronounced "brim" down south. His other names are blackear bream, blue bream, blue Joe, bluemouthed sunfish, blue perch, blue sunfish, copperhead bream, coppernosed bream, coppernosed sunfish, dollardee, polladee, and sun perch.

In color the bluegill has a blue-green to olive-green back becoming lighter on the sides. The breast is orange-yellow or orange-red. The younger specimens usually have vertical bars on the sides. Older and larger bluegills often have a dark purplish back, a dull orange breast and may lack the vertical stripes. It can usually be distinguished from other sunfish by its dark ear

BLUEGILL

The bluegill has delighted countless youngsters like this young boy. It is often the first fish caught by kids and many continue to fish for them through life. Here five-year-old Billy Smith admires his "sunny." (PHOTO BY JOHNNY NICKLAS, PENNSYLVANIA FISH COMMISSION)

flap on the lower end of the gill cover and a dark blotch on the lower end of the second dorsal fin.

More bluegills are probably caught on cane poles, glass poles, and poles cut from saplings or branches of trees than any other tackle. The cane or glass pole from 10 to 20 feet long is still a popular fishing tool and is used by many bluegill fishermen. A light monofilament line testing about 6 or 8 pounds is tied to the end and a small or thin float or bobber is slipped on the line. The hook can be a size No. 6, 8, or 10 and is tied to the end of the line. This outfit is usually used with some kind of live or natural bait on the hook.

Spinning rods and reels in the lighter weights also make ideal bluegill fishing outfits. For bait-fishing you can use your regular fresh-water spinning rod. For casting small lures an ultralight rod and reel with thin lines testing only about 2 pounds are ideal.

Many anglers believe that a bluegill should only be caught on a fly rod. The shorter, lighter fly rods about 7, 7½ or at the most 8 feet long are best. The fly reel, either single-action or the automatic type, can be filled with monofilament line or about 6-pound test for bait fishing. For casting flies or tiny lures a regular fly line is better.

Lures which can be used for bluegills include the dry flies such as the Wulff flies, bi-visibles, Gray Hackle, Black Gnat, and other trout flies in sizes 8, 10, 12, or 14. Wet flies such as the Coachman, Black Ant, McGinty, White Miller, Brown Hackle, and other patterns can be used. Sizes No. 8, 10, 12, and 14 should be carried. The larger ones are best for the big bluegills while the smaller ones should be used for the smaller fish. Various small bass bugs and panfish bugs such as the poppers are very good. So are the sponge or rubber bodied spiders with long rubber legs. These come in floating and sinking types. Black, white, yellow, and brown are favorite colors. Nymphs of various sizes, colors, and patterns are also great bluegill lures. So are the smaller streamers and bucktails. Bluegills will also strike the smaller spoons, spinners, and tiny plugs at times.

In natural baits the most popular bluegill bait is the earthworm. Night crawlers aren't as good as the smaller varieties of worms. They'll also take tiny minnows about an inch and a half in length at times. Insects such as grasshoppers, crickets, roaches, catalpa worms, mealworms, corn borers, and grubs also make fine bluegill baits. If you run out of bait try a tiny strip of pork rind, piece of bread or dough, or a small chunk cut from a bluegill or other fish.

The fastest bluegill fishing takes place in the late spring or early summer when they are spawning or have just finished guarding their nests. Then they are easy to locate and are pugnacious and hungry. But they bite most of the

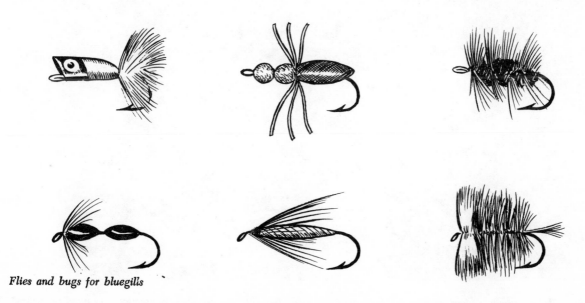

Flies and bugs for bluegills

summer and into the late fall. You can catch them all day long with bait or sunken lures. For fly fishing, the early morning, late afternoon and evening hours are best.

When bluegills are spawning they are easy to locate since they are close to shore over their nests which are circular and stand out against the rest of the bottom. At others times, they frequent weed beds, submerged logs, sunken trees, rocks, brush, lily pads, pilings and docks. In the summer the bigger bluegills may move out to deeper water and hang around the drop-offs, edges of steep banks and the deep water around rocky points and sand bars. Most bluegills are caught in water from 2 to 15 feet deep, but in some lakes the big ones may drop down to about 30 or 40 feet in the middle of the day. In the evening you can often see bluegills dimpling the surface as they pick insects off the top.

Most bluegills are caught still fishing from shore, bridges, piers, docks, and boats. Here you can fish with or without a bobber and drop your bait into likely spots. But don't set the hook too fast since bluegills and other sunfish have small mouths. Give them plenty of time to swallow the bait and start moving away with it. A float is usually more fun because you can watch it bob up and down, then when it is pulled under you can set the hook. Use the smallest and lightest float you can get for bluegills.

Some of the larger bluegills are smart and wary and take off when you get too close. For them, a spinning rod is ideal because you can usually cast your bobber or float with a tiny clincher sinker on the leader and the bait a good distance. So instead of approaching too close you can cast from shore or a boat to a good spot and let the bait stay there. The first big splash

Bluegills are usually caught near shore. Areas with lily pads like this one are often productive. (PERKINS OUTBOARD MOTORS)

Combination float or plug and bug or fly

may chase the bluegills away but they'll soon return and investigate the bait. It is also a good idea to jerk the bait or move it every so often to keep it from hiding in the weeds and also to attract the attention of the fish.

When bluegills are inclined to take fly lures off the surface a lot of fun can be had by wading in the water along the shoreline or moving in a boat some distance from land. Then you cast small dry flies or tiny panfish bugs into likely looking spots. Drop the fly close to logs, rocks, stumps, lily pads, and let it lie there a minute or two. Then twitch it gently so it moves a few inches. Then let it lie a few seconds more, then twitch it once again. Keep doing this until the lure is too far away from where the fish are. Dry flies or small bugs are best in the evening and when the water is calm.

During the middle of the day and when the water is ruffled, a wet fly, nymph, or tiny streamer is better. One of these can be tried first without any weight a few inches to a couple of feet below the surface. It should be retrieved very slowly in short jerks. If no results are forthcoming try sinking the lure still deeper. To save time you can add a couple of split-shot to the leader above the fly.

The same thing can be done with small lures such as spoons, spinners, tiny plugs, and jigs.

Try different depths and work the lure as slowly as possible. In clear water you can often see the bluegill chase and grab the lure.

One of the most effective rigs for bluegills to use with a casting or spinning outfit is a combination plastic float and small panfish bug behind it on a short leader. You can't cast a small bug alone, but the plastic float provides enough weight to carry the bug to its destination. Instead of the plastic float you can substitute a small surface plug or a weighted bass bug. The 6- or 8-pound test leader from the float or weight can be about 12 or 14 inches long. The panfish bug or dry fly is tied to the end of this leader. (See illustration.)

When using this combinaton rig you cast to the spot and let it lie there for a minute or so, then give it a short jerk. The float, plug, or weight makes a small splash while the fly or bug behind makes a ripple. Then let it lie still again after which you jerk or twitch it once more. Keep doing this until a bluegill comes up and grabs the small bug or fly. Sometimes a big bass will come up and grab the plug ahead of the smaller lure.

A bluegill hooked on light tackle puts up a very satisfactory fight. It is usually short because the bluegill and other sunfish lack the staying power of the larger game fishes. But it is spirited and lively while it lasts with a good-sized bluegill making circle after circle.

In most bodies of water a half-pound bluegill is a good one and a fish around a pound is a big one. In some lakes bluegills and other sunfish may become stunted and never reach a good size. In other lakes they grow larger than average if conditions are suitable. Such as Ketona Lake in Alabama where bluegills over 4 pounds in weight have been caught. The largest weighed 4 pounds 12 ounces and was taken by T. S. Hudson on April 9, 1950.

Large or small, bluegills and other sunfish make excellent eating. Their meat is firm, sweet, and delicious. It takes some time and trouble to clean the smaller bluegills or sunfish. So many anglers save only the larger ones or fish in lakes or rivers where big ones are commonly caught. But fishery biologists frown on this practice and would much rather have all anglers take as many bluegills of all sizes as often as they can. There are just too many bluegills and other sunfishes in many lakes and ponds and they should be thinned out as often as possible. Then those that are remaining will grow larger and so will the game fish which need plenty of living space and food.

Chapter 18

CRAPPIES

The crappie is one of the more popular panfishes especially on the larger lakes and reservoirs where it is found. Big catches are made because they are fairly easy to catch and gather in large schools. The season for crappie fishing is long in many areas, starting in March and continuing up to November. They are even caught through the ice during the winter months. When crappies are running it is not unusual to see a hundred or more boats congregated over the crappie beds on the larger lakes. In addition to the boat fishermen, hundreds of other anglers line the piers, banks, and shorelines to catch crappies.

There are two kinds of crappies—the black crappie and the white crappie. The black crappie is deeper bodied, has a black back and is darkly mottled. It has seven or eight dorsal spines. The white crappie is not so deep-bodied or so dark as the black crappie. It is much lighter in color and has five or six dorsal spines.

Crappies are called by almost sixty different names but the more popular ones are calico bass, speckled perch, strawberry bass, silver crappie, and bachelor.

The black crappie is more numerous in northern waters than the white crappie and is found from southern Canada, through the Great Lakes and Mississippi River system, to Nebraska and south to Texas, Florida, and North Carolina. The white crappie which is most plentiful in southern waters is found from Nebraska to Lake Ontario and south to the Mississippi River, Texas, and Alabama. Both crappies, however, have been introduced widely in other states and waters as far west as California, Oregon, and Washington.

Fishing tackle used for crappies is similar to that used for other panfishes. Cane poles and glass poles are popular with many fishermen from boats or shore. They are particularly useful when fishing around brush, sunken trees, logs,

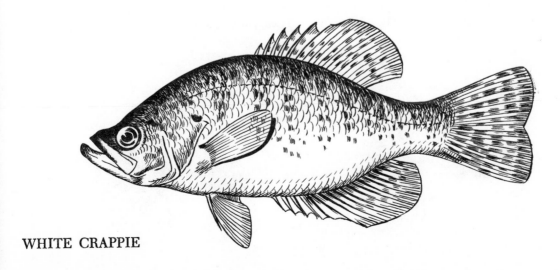

WHITE CRAPPIE

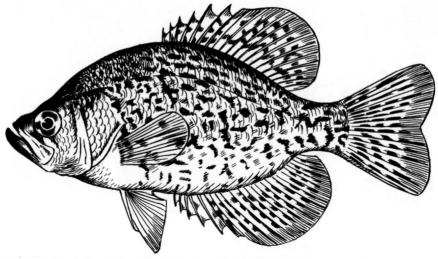

BLACK CRAPPIE

and weeds where the bait can be lowered in the holes between such snags. Bait-casting rods and reels are good for casting or trolling. And, of course, spinning rods and reels and spin-casting tackle can be used for casting small lures and also for still fishing and trolling. Fly rods are great for fishing for crappies when they are in shallow water.

Crappies will strike such artificial lures as small underwater plugs, tiny spoons, weighted spinners, spinners and flies, or bait and small jigs. Fly fishermen can catch them with small streamers and bucktails, wet flies, nymphs, dry flies, and bass bugs or panfish bugs. In recent years the small jigs which have weighted heads and bodies of chenille and marabou tails have become popular for jigging and casting for crappies. (See illustration.)

Natural baits which will catch crappies include minnows, worms, grasshoppers, mealworms, crickets, nymphs, and other insects. But the most dependable bait is a small minnow from 1½ to 2½ inches long. After you catch the first crappie you can cut a strip from its silvery sides or belly and use it for bait. Strips about ¼ inch wide and 1½ inches long can be cut from other fish such as suckers, chubs, gizzard shad, etc., and used for bait.

Crappies may start running as early as February or March in our southern states and fishing may continue until June. In more northern waters the best months are usually April, May, and June. During the summer months they go into deeper water and are harder to locate and catch. Then fishing picks up again in the fall and often

Jigs used for crappies

lasts until winter. But they can also be caught through the ice during the cold months.

In the spring crappies gather in shallow water near shore to spawn and are easy to locate. You'll usually see fleets of boats congregated over the crappie beds. As a general rule, black crappies prefer clearer, cooler waters than the white crappies which are often found in warmer, sluggish muddier waters. Both species like to hang out in coves, bays, around old stumps, boulders, brush, sunken trees, lily pads, hyacinths, and other weeds and vegetation. During floods look for them in flooded pasture lands, coves, and inlets. When the water is muddy they'll be in the clearer areas near shore. During the summer months they are in the deeper holes in shady spots under overhanging trees, bridges, piers, rafts, anchored boats, and lily pads. In spring and fall they may be in water as shallow as 3 to 8 feet but in the hot summer months you may have to seek them in depths up to 20 or even 30 feet.

Still fishing is the most popular way to catch crappies and the long cane or glass pole is generally used. With this pole the crappie rig illustrated here is often used. This makes use of a stopper which is usually a short stick or button attached on the leader or line to approximate the depth of the water being fished. Then a sliding cork is slipped on the leader below the stopper. Next a small sliding sinker is slipped on below the cork. Finally a small hook about size No. 3 or 4 is tied to the end of the leader. This is baited with a small minnow and is lowered into likely holes and spots where crappies are found. The sinker takes the bait straight down to the bottom and the cork slides up to the stopper. In shallow water a fixed float or bobber which doesn't slide but can be adjusted at any depth can be used.

Usually crappies stay at a certain level when feeding and it is important to find out what this is if you want to get action. Try different depths until you find the one at which they are feeding. And give them plenty of time to swallow the minnow before you set the hook.

When casting lures such as small spoons, weighted spinners, small plugs, and jigs for crappies the same exploring of different depths is necessary. Sometimes the fish will be in shallow water near shore and then the lure can be retrieved near the surface. Other times they will be down deep and then the lure should be allowed to sink well down before you start reeling back. Cast the lures as close to brush piles, stumps, logs, lily pads as possible. And retrieve as slowly as possible to give the crappies time to catch up to the lure and grab it.

When fishing in waters with many obstructions jigging will often work better than casting. Here,

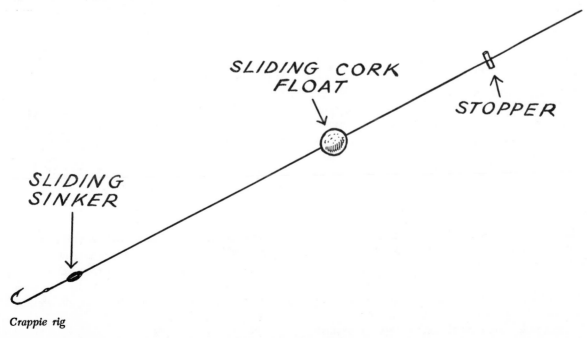

SLIDING CORK
FLOAT

STOPPER

SLIDING
SINKER

Crappie rig

Big strings of crappies are often taken from the larger lakes, rivers and reservoirs in the South. (TENNESSEE GAME AND FISH COMMISSION)

you merely lower a small yellow or white jig to the bottom under the boat and work it up and down.

In more open waters trolling is often a good way to locate and catch crappies. A slow-moving boat following the shoreline around points of land, along bars, weed beds, and coves and channels will take them. You can let out about 75 or 100 feet of line and use small spinners and minnows, tiny underwater plugs and spoons on the end. In shallow water no weight is usually needed but in deep water a trolling rig with a three-way swivel and a sinker may be required to get down near the bottom.

When crappies come into the shallows in the evening to feed on the surface on insects you can sometimes catch them with a fly rod. For this, dry flies and small bass bugs or panfish bugs are best. Work them slowly with plenty of pauses and twitches to bring the crappies to the top.

It would be dishonest to say that the crappie is a great fighter on the end of a line. They usually wage a slow, uninteresting short fight and give up too quickly. In addition, they have soft, paper-tissue mouths and a hook will often pull out or drop out. So light tackle is best in getting the most out of them and for saving the most fish that are hooked.

Crappies in most waters will average about a pound or a bit less. However, in some lakes and reservoirs they are often caught up to 2 or 3 pounds in weight. Both species of crappies reach about 5 pounds or slightly more in weight and a length of about 20 inches.

Crappies are often caught by cane-pole and bobber fishermen when they come into shallow water near shore. (JOHN-
SON MOTORS PHOTO)

The crappie is one of the best panfish when it comes to eating.

They are especially good in the early spring or late fall and during the winter months when the flesh is firm. Those taken from muddy waters and during the hot summer months may be softer and not so well flavored.

Some of the better crappie lakes and rivers are found in Wisconsin, Iowa, Idaho, Minnesota, Oklahoma, Pennsylvania, and many of the states bordering the Mississippi River. In New York, Chautauqua Lake and Lake Ontario are noted for crappie fishing. In Mississippi the Enid Reservoir has some big crappies. In Tennessee, Kentucky Lake and Reelfoot Lake have good crappie fishing. In Texas, Lake Buchanan, Lake Travis, Lake Belton, Lake Texarkana, and the Highland Lakes chain as well as many other man-made lakes and reservoirs have them. In Florida, Lake Okeechobee, Lake Apopka, Lake Eustis, Lake Dora, Lake Harris, and the St. John's River are good crappie waters. On the Pacific Coast in Oregon the Columbia River and Willamette River sloughs, Owyhee, Cold Springs, Fern Ridge, Coffenbury, Smith, and Siltcoos Lakes have been stocked with crappies.

Chapter 19

WHITE BASS

How would you like to catch a fresh-water fish that runs bigger than the average panfish, fights harder, strikes many kinds of artificial lures, and makes delicious eating? And when these fish are really running it's a cinch to catch the limit. Many of you are probably already familiar with this fish, but those who are not should become acquainted with this silvery little scrapper. He's the white bass also called the silver bass, barfish, gray bass, sand bass, silversides, striper, and striped bass. But the last two names are better reserved for his relative—the salt-water striped bass which grows much larger and is a more streamlined fish. The white bass is shorter, broader, and much smaller, and strictly a fresh-water fish. His back is greenish, the sides are silvery and six or seven stripes run along the sides.

Unfortunately, because of limited distribution, the white bass is known mostly to the anglers in the central part of the United States. Otherwise, this fish would be one of the top favorites in the country occupying a position somewhere between the panfishes and the black bass. At present the white bass ranges from New York through the Great Lakes to Minnesota, south to Texas and east to Alabama and Tennessee. They prefer large rivers and lakes and are very plentiful in man-made lakes and reservoirs in the TVA system in Tennessee and in Texas. They are common in the Mississippi River and its tributaries.

For casting light lures for white bass the ideal outfit is a light fresh-water spinning rod and reel. The line should be about 4- or 6-pound test monofilament and the rod should be able to

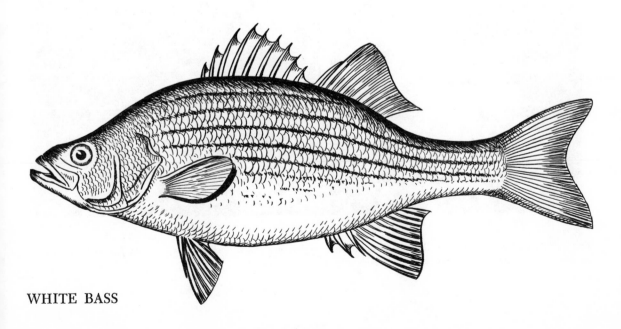

WHITE BASS

Bag limits on white bass are usually very generous and anglers are encouraged to take as many fish as is legal. (TEN-NESSEE CONSERVATION DEPARTMENT)

cast lures ranging from ⅛ to ½ ounce. The spin-casting rods with push-button type reels are also good for casting.

If you prefer a bait-casting outfit get the lightest one, about 5½ or 6 feet long and able to cast the light lures used. Lines testing about 8 or 10 pounds should be used with such a rod. If you use a heavier rod and line you'll have trouble casting the small lures required in white bass fishing. However, the heavier bait-casting outfits would be good for trolling or bottom fishing with bait.

When white bass are actively feeding they'll strike almost anything which moves through the water and even remotely resembles a minnow. They'll take small surface and underwater plugs, spoons, spinners, streamer and bucktail flies, and weighted jigs of all types. The important fact to remember is that the lure you use should be small. The big plugs and spoons used for black bass and other large fish are not too good. The white bass has a small mouth and you'll miss too many fish if you use large lures.

If you have no outfit capable of casting very light and small lures you can get around this by making up a "popping block" or "chugging block" to give you added weight. This can be a small section of broomstick or dowel anywhere from 2 to 3 inches long. Two small screw eyes are fastened to both ends of this block. Your fishing line is tied to one screw eye and a 2-foot monofilament leader is tied to the other eye. To the end of the leader you can attach a tiny spoon, bucktail or streamer fly or jig. When this is cast and reeled in, the wooden block creates a commotion and acts as a fish attractor besides providing weight for casting. It may be a bit clumsy to cast at first but it gets a light lure out much farther.

The peak season for white bass fishing is in the spring when they run up creeks to spawn. This may start as early as March in some of the southern states or in April, May, or June farther north. During the summer months good fishing can often be had on some of the larger reservoirs and lakes.

The best time to fish is when the white bass are actually chasing small gizzard shad or minnows on the surface of the lake. Calm days are best for locating them. Other times the best fish-ing usually takes place early in the morning and in the evening. They can also be caught at night in many waters.

When white bass are chasing small fish on the surface they often churn the water to a froth and the commotion can be spotted a long distance away. In some places, such as Lake Erie, gulls and terns congregate over such feeding white bass and pinpoint the fish for you. Other times look for white bass in the fast water below dams and around piers, breakwaters, and jetties. In rivers they prefer the swifter bends and holes. In lakes, fish around rocky points, inlets, sand and rock bars, and deep water near shore. But white bass tend to wander all over the lake or reservoir and you either try to follow them from spot to spot, or you wait in one spot and hope they will pass by a few times during the day.

Because of their habit of chasing gizzard shad and minnows to the surface, white bass fishing on some of the larger bodies of water calls for quick action. Anglers cruise around in their boats with their rods rigged and look for feeding schools of fish. As soon as they spot a commotion they speed toward that spot. When they get within casting distance they cut their motors and everybody starts casting small spoons, plugs, jigs, or chugging blocks. Fast reeling usually produces the best results at this time. You have only a short time before the school sounds or is frightened by too many boats. Then you have to locate another school or wait till the fish reappear. This is exciting sport known as "jump" fishing but it can become hectic with too many boats trying to get in on the act.

Some anglers prefer to troll for their white bass even when the fish are surfacing. At such times fast trolling up to 5 or 6 miles an hour with the lure a short distance behind the boat will catch them. Other times a slower-moving boat with a long line is better. When there are no white bass showing, deep trolling will often take them. Then you have to use weights or sinkers on your line to get the lure down. Spinners and minnows, small underwater plugs, spoons and jigs can all be used when trolling.

White bass can also be caught by still fishing with live minnows when they are down deep. Small minnows between 2 and 2½ inches long

Many lakes and reservoirs in Tennessee offer good white bass fishing. This is Watts Bar Lake. (PAUL A. MOORE, TENNESSEE CONSERVATION DEPARTMENT)

are best for this fishing. This is often a very productive method at night. To attract minnows and white bass you hang one or two lanterns or lights on the boat so that they shine into the water. This is also a good way to catch fresh bait. The minnows gather below the light and you can scoop them up with a dip net. The minnow is impaled on a small hook and is lowered anywhere from 20 to 50 feet down. Give the fish plenty of time to swallow the minnow before you set the hook.

White bass put up a good scrap for their size and have more endurance than most panfish. They do most of their fighting below the surface and don't leap. But on light tackle they are a lot of fun.

White bass don't grow too big, but average from ¾ to 2 pounds in weight which is still larger than the average panfish. Fish weighing 4 and 5 pounds or a bit more have been caught from time to time in various waters.

However, the white bass is so prolific and has such a short life span that most states have liberal bag limits on them. Most of them live only three or four years and if not caught they die and are wasted. So biologists claim that it's a good idea to catch your limit as often as you can. And when they are really running this is no feat. If you can't give them away to your neighbors, try cleaning or filleting them and putting them in the deep-freeze, if you have one. They make good eating, having a firm, tasty flesh.

White bass fishing is best in the deep South where the season is long and the fish large and plentiful. In such states as Texas you'll find them in Lake Texoma, Travis, Buchanan, Marshall Ford, Caddo, Dallas, and the Rio Grande. In Tennessee most of the man-made reservoirs and lakes have white bass with Kentucky Lake and Watts Bar Reservoir offering good fishing. In Kentucky, Dix River, Herrington Lake, Lake Cumberland, Dale Hollow Lake, and many other lakes and rivers contain white bass. In Missouri, the Lake of the Ozarks and Bull Shoals are noted for this fishing. In Arkansas, Lake Hamilton and Ouachita River are fished. In South Carolina, you'll find white bass in the Catawba River and in the Santee-Cooper waters. In Wisconsin, Lake Mendota is well known for its white bass fishing. In Illinois you'll find them in the Illinois River, Lake Chautauqua, Quiver Lake, and Lake Matanzas. In New York they are found in Oneida Lake and the St. Lawrence River. White bass are also found in most of the Great Lakes with the exception of Lake Superior where they are rare or missing. White bass are constantly being stocked in many other states and waters.

Chapter 20

WHITE PERCH

The white perch is a panfish like the sunfishes, crappies, yellow perch, rock bass, and others in this class. But he's a neglected or overlooked panfish among most outdoor writers and many anglers. You rarely read about them in books or magazines, and few anglers go fishing deliberately for white perch. Yet the white perch has many qualities which make him popular with some fresh-water anglers who rate him over most of the other panfishes.

The white perch is not related to the yellow perch or the perch family for that matter. He's a member of the sea bass family which includes the white bass and the salt-water striped bass. He resembles both of these fish in general outline but does not have the stripes. In color the upper surface varies depending on where he's found. But it is usually an olive or dark grayish-green or silver-gray on the back and upper sides. These colors shade into a paler olive or silvery

green to silvery white on the belly. When found in fresh water it is usually much darker than when found in brackish or salt waters.

The white perch is found from Nova Scotia down to the Carolinas mostly in rivers, creeks, salt-water ponds, and bays near the Atlantic Ocean. They have also been introduced into many fresh-water lakes and ponds in the eastern states. But their natural habitat are the rivers emptying into the sea and salt-water and brackish ponds formed by being cut off from the ocean by sand bars. These ponds usually "salt out" in time and become mostly fresh water.

White perch can be caught on various kinds of outfits from cane poles to light salt-water rods and reels. When fishing in quiet ponds or creeks near shore an ordinary cane pole would do the trick nicely and can be used with or without a float or bobber When they are in shallow water near shore a fly rod also makes a sporting outfit

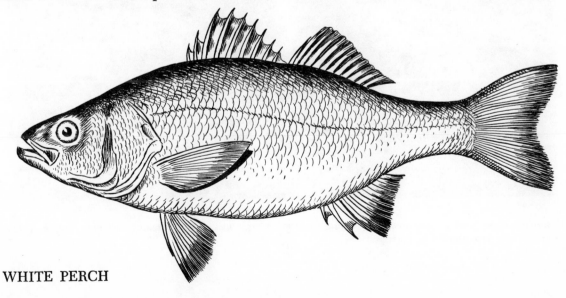

WHITE PERCH

If there are white perch in your area the youngsters will get a great kick out of catching this tasty panfish. (DELA-WARE BOARD OF FISH AND GAME COMMISSIONERS)

for these fish. When casting is required a light fresh-water spinning outfit or bait-casting outfit can be used. In brackish or salt-water with strong currents and tides and when fishing among rocks, a heavier salt-water spinning rod and reel or salt-water spinning rod and reel or salt-water conventional rod and reel can be used.

The white perch will often hit artificial lures such as wet flies or streamer flies used on a fly rod. Those with silver bodies are especially good. Other effective lures include small spoons and weighted spinners. For trolling a small spinner rigged ahead of a garden worm is often used.

In the natural bait line white perch will take earthworms and night crawlers. Minnows and baby eels are very good for them too. So are various kinds of insects such as grasshoppers, crickets, and grubs. Soft-shell crayfish in the smaller sizes are also used at times. In brackish and salt water they can be caught on grass shrimp, bloodworms, sandworms, and pieces of shedder crab.

White perch can be caught from early spring to late fall in most waters where they are found. They spend the winter in deep water or brackish bays, then move into rivers and creeks to spawn in April and May. They often run up big rivers into fresh water many miles from the sea.

You can catch white perch pretty well during the daytime, although they might be in deeper water at that time. You can also catch them at dusk and at night and when fishing is usually better near shore when they come into shallow water to feed.

White perch seem to prefer medium deep water much of the time and are usually found in fresh-water in depths from 8 to 20 feet. However in some deep fresh-water lakes and in big salt-water bays like the Chesapeake they may be anywhere from 30 to 100 feet down.

The white perch is also a pretty adaptable fish, and hardy fish being able to live in warm and cold waters and in waters of wide salinity, range from fresh to salt. However, it prefers brackish waters of bays, sounds, lagoons, tidal creeks, and river mouths. It may be found over mud, clay, sand, or rocky bottoms. The white

perch are usually found in schools numbering from a few to several thousand fish.

Early in the morning or toward evening when the lake is calm you can often see schools of white perch close to the surface. At such times they may be showing their backs or even breaking water. If they are merely swimming around you may not be able to get them to hit a bait or lure. But if they are feeding on insects or chasing minnows you can often get some action.

Still fishing with a cane or glass pole near shore or in shallow creeks is a popular way to catch white perch. Since they start feeding early in the spring soon after the ice is out they attract many anglers at that time. You can use a bobber or float above your hook, and bait it with one of the natural baits mentioned above.

In fast rivers or when trying to reach a spot some distance away from shore a casting outfit like a spinning rod is better. Here you can use a standard bottom rig with a small sinker tied on the end of the line and a hook on a short snell or leader above it. This can be baited with a worm or minnow and can be cast out from shore. You can put your rod in a holder or against a log or rock on the bank and then wait for a bite. They bite with vigor but because of their small mouths, time must be given for them to mouth the bait before you set the hook.

At times the white perch will take artificial lures and then you can cast for them with small spoons, spinners, or spinner and worm combinations. These can be worked near the surface if the fish are on top. Or you can let them sink down close to the bottom and work the lures slowly toward the surface.

They'll also take fly rod lures such as wet flies and small streamers in the gaudier patterns with silver bodies. These should also be worked at different depths and speeds of retrieve to find out what they want.

White perch put up a much better fight on the end of the line than the yellow perch or rock bass. The big ones, especially when hooked in a river with a strong current or in salt water where a strong tide is running will often put up a long, spirited battle. However, the tackle must be light for them to show their best since they are small fish.

The average white perch caught runs from 8

to 10 inches long and weighs less than a pound. In some lakes and brackish waters fish going 2 or 3 pounds may be caught. One of the largest caught was a 19½ inch white perch weighing close to 5 pounds. This was taken in Messalonskee Lake, Maine, by Mrs. Earl Small.

The white perch makes excellent eating when cleaned and fried in deep fat. It has a firm, flaky, sweet-tasting flesh and the big ones can be filleted. You can also make a delicious chowder from them. In the early spring or late fall when the females have eggs or roe, you can remove these, dip them in flour and egg and fry them.

You can go for white perch in Canada, in Nova Scotia, and in New Brunswick. In Maine they are found in the Belgrade chain of lakes, in Messalonskee Lake and many other lakes and ponds. In Massachusetts, Rhode Island, and Connecticut many lakes, ponds, and rivers have these fish. In New York you'll find white perch in many waters on Long Island and upstate in the reservoirs and large lakes. They are very plentiful in the Hudson River in salt and brackish water. In New Jersey, you can fish the Hudson River, Delaware River, Toms River, and many lakes and ponds. In Virginia and Maryland the Chesapeake Bay and its tributaries contain many white perch.

Chapter 21

ROCK BASS

The rock bass is one of those fish which doesn't get much publicity in the outdoor columns of newspapers or in magazines or books. In fact, most anglers seem to ignore this fish and rarely brag about catching rock bass. That's probably because very few anglers deliberately fish for rock bass. This fish is usually caught while an angler is seeking black bass, walleyes, or some other fish.

Yet the rock bass is a worthy little panfish which can provide some excellent sport and fine eating afterward. He is a very willing biter and is usually easy to catch. He's found in almost two thirds of the United States from the Great Lakes to the St. Lawrence River west to the Dakotas and south to the Gulf of Mexico and Florida. He has been introduced widely and is

found in many states in the East where he formerly was missing.

The rock bass is a member of the sunfish family and resembles the sunfishes in general outline and shape. But the rock bass has a much larger mouth than any sunfish and a red eye. The back is olive-green to black and blends into a yellow or bronze on the sides. There are dark patches of scales which give the fish a mottled effect on each side. The belly is yellowish white.

The rock bass is also called the goggle-eye, redeye, sun perch, lake bass, sunfish bass, frogmouth perch, rock sunfish, redeye sunfish, redeye bream, and redeye perch.

Many rock bass are caught by youngsters with cane poles or glass poles about 10 or 12 feet long. These can be used with or without a bobber

ROCK BASS

This rock bass won't pull that scale down much but he offers some sport when other fish won't bite. These fish prefer the slower moving portions of rivers and are usually caught on worms. (OHIO DEPARTMENT OF NATURAL RESOURCES)

above the hook. A light or ultralight spinning outfit or spin-casting outfit is good for bait fishing or casting lures. And a fly rod as always will provide the maximum sport with rock bass.

Rock bass will hit spinner and fly or spinner and bait combinations when cast and reeled slowly. The wingless or hackle flies should be used behind a spinner. They'll also strike small underwater and surface plugs. Weighted spinners and small spoons can also be tried. Fly rod anglers can use bass bugs or panfish bugs, streamers and bucktails, and wet flies. The more colorful, gaudier patterns of flies will work as well if not better than the darker, somber patterns.

However, most rock bass are caught on natural baits such as worms, hellgrammites, insects, and minnows. Small crayfish about 1½ or 2 inches long are the best size to use. Minnows should also be about 2 or 2½ inches long.

The season for rock bass is long because this fish starts to bite early in the spring and continues late into the fall. In the colder creeks and rivers he will often bite all summer long when smallmouthed bass or trout refuse to co-operate. And he bites almost as well at night as during the daytime.

As the name implies the rock bass loves to hang out around rocks and that's where to look for him. He is found in rivers and streams with rocky or gravel bottoms. In rivers look for him under overhanging banks, under rock ledges, under trees, bushes, logs—almost anywhere he can find cover and shade. Rock bass in rivers usually stay out of the main currents and fastest water. Instead they prefer the quieter pools, backwaters, and eddies. In lakes, you'll find them around lily pads, stumps, pilings, docks, piers, submerged logs, trees, and along rocky shores. The big rock bass in rivers will often be found in the tails of pools and in the eddies, below dams and around bridge supports and sunken trees. Look for them on the upstream side of obstructions waiting for the lazy current to bring them food. They are usually in shallow water in the morning, evening, and at night. In the daytime they are hidden in shady spots or in deeper water.

When still fishing with bait it's a good idea to keep the bait moving slowly with the current into spots where the rock bass may be lying. One method is to wade in the water and drop your bait into likely spots. You can use a bobber in deeper water but this is not necessary in shallow water.

When using lures such as small plugs, spoons, spinners, or spinner and fly combinations you can cast down and across stream, let the lure swing with the current and then slowly bring it back close to the bottom. Wet flies and streamers can be used the same way. Bass bugs and dry flies can be popped or twitched in short jerks on the surface. The evening and nighttime are usually best for fly fishing when the rock bass are in the shallows near shore and feeding on insects.

Small rock bass swarm all over and are often found in schools and are easy to catch. The bigger rock bass are more wary, more solitary, and more likely to be found in deeper water. To catch them you have to approach their hiding spots carefully and make fairly long casts.

Unfortunately, rock bass are feeble fighters on the end of a line and give up rather quickly. A good-sized fish in a fast current or in snag-infested waters may provide a few thrills on light tackle.

Most rock bass caught will range from about 4 to 8 inches in length and weigh about ½ pound or a bit less. Some waters may contain good-sized fish up to a pound or a bit more in weight. They may reach slightly more than 2 pounds in southern waters. A 2½ pound rock bass was reported from the Stone's River in Tennessee.

Rock bass make good eating if taken early or late in the year from cold, clean water. Those taken from lakes and ponds or slow moving, muddy waters especially during the summer months, may be soft and have a muddy flavor. This can be avoided to some extent if the big ones are skinned or filleted.

We won't list any waters where rock bass are found because most anglers will continue to fish for other species and take the rock bass if they happen to come across them. Most anglers catch them in rivers when fishing for smallmouthed bass or in lakes and ponds when fishing for largemouthed bass or other panfish.

Chapter 22

CATFISH

Fishing for catfish is very popular in waters where these dark, smooth bewhiskered fish are numerous. Down South, for example, on our larger rivers and lakes and reservoirs you'll often see the banks lined by hundreds of eager catfish anglers seeking these fish. Additional hundreds will be out in small boats dangling their lines near the bottom hoping a big catfish will come along and engulf the bait. Even in northern waters where channel catfish were stocked in certain lakes they have proven more popular than black bass.

Catfish are sought by thousands of fresh-water anglers because they often come big and make delicious eating. Also, they are found in warmer, muddier waters and near cities where trout, bass, and other delicate game fish have tough going. They also bite well at night and many a working angler does a bit of catfishing after din-

ner in the evening and night without missing a day's work.

When we talk about catfish we must mention the fact that there are at least twenty-four species found in North America. But of these we are mainly concerned here with four: the blue catfish, channel catfish, white catfish, and flathead catfish. Of these, the biggest is the blue catfish which is also called the chucklehead, great blue catfish, great forktail catfish, and Mississippi blue catfish. This catfish is gray or dusky blue on the back with a silvery white belly. The tail is deeply forked. It is the largest of the catfish found in the United States sometimes reaching 150 pounds or more.

The channel catfish resembles the blue catfish but is more streamlined and reaches a smaller size. It is also known as the squealer, willow catfish, fiddler, forktail catfish, speckled catfish, and

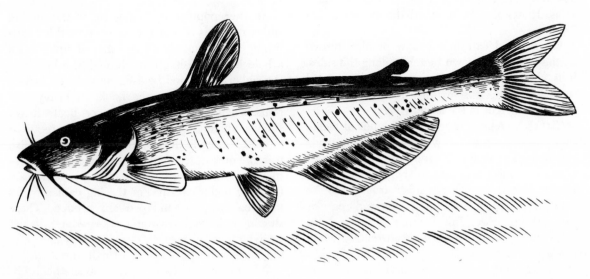

CATFISH

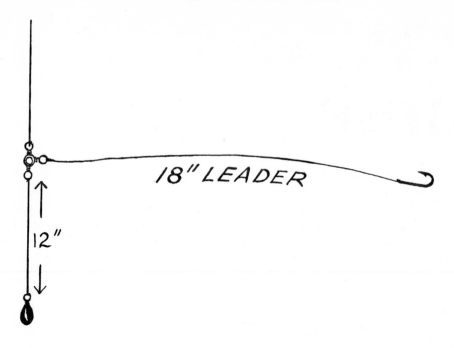

18" LEADER

12"

Catfish rig

silver catfish. It is usually gray or grayish blue on top, with a silvery tinge and black spots along the sides. The tail is deeply forked. It may reach 50 pounds or more in weight.

The white catfish is pale olive or blue-gray on top and white on the belly. The tail is forked but not so deeply as in the channel catfish. It may reach 60 pounds in weight in certain waters but rarely goes over 15 pounds in most areas. It has also been called the Potomac catfish.

The flathead catfish is yellow or olive-brown on the back with brown blotches along the sides. It is also called the yellow cat, mud cat, and shovelhead cat. It sometimes reaches over 100 pounds in weight in the larger rivers.

Catfish have been caught on all kinds of tackle from simple drop or throw lines to deep-sea rods and reels. The ordinary cane pole is often used when the catfish are close to shore or in narrow creeks. For the smaller catfish from 2 to 15 pounds you can use spinning rods and reels or bait-casting tackle. But for the big catfish in large rivers and where strong currents prevail, you need heavier outfits. For boat fishing a salt-water boat rod and reel will serve the purpose. For fishing from shore where long casts may be

required the shorter conventional and spinning surf rods are often put to use.

Various types of rigs are employed in catfishing. When fishing in quiet waters the hook is merely tied to the end of the line and the bait is cast out and allowed to sink. But when distance is needed a sinker is added to the end of the line and the hook is tied a few inches above it.

Another popular catfishing rig is the sliding sinker rig. This is similar to the one used for carp fishing and is merely an egg-shaped sinker with a hole in it. The line runs through the hole and the sinker is stopped by a barrel swivel attached about two feet above the hook. In heavy currents when fishing from shore or boats heavy sinkers up to 8 or 10 ounces may be required to hold bottom in deep water. But in most catfish waters you can use much lighter weights. Hooks in sizes 1/0, 2/0, 3/0, and 4/0 are usually used for the smaller catfish. For the big catfish hooks in sizes 7/0, 8/0 and 9/0 are needed. These should be strong, salt-water types which do not straighten too easily. The Eagle Claw and O'Shaughnessy patterns are usually favored.

When it comes to baits for catfish the list is long and varied. Earthworms such as garden

The channel catfish is a game fighter on rod and reel and is often found in fast rivers as well as lakes. Bait used for this one was a soft-shelled crayfish. (PHOTO BY JOHNNY NICKLAS, PENNSYLVANIA FISH COMMISSION)

worms and night crawlers are tops and up to a dozen or more of the smaller ones may be needed on a single hook. Another good bait is a fresh-water clam or mussel which is opened and the meat allowed to stand for a day or two to ripen. Various chunks and strips of meat such as beef, lamb, pork, poultry can be used. The heart, liver, and lungs of such animals can also be tried. The guts, too, from the smaller animals such as rabbits, poultry and fish such as carp and buffalo are good. For big catfish small dead birds, mice, chicks, and frogs can be used. For smaller catfish, insects such as grasshoppers, catalpa worms, locusts, and grubs can be drifted in the currents during the summer months. An excellent bait is a soft-shelled crayfish tied on to a hook.

Various kinds of small fishes and minnows can also be used in catfishing. In Tennessee and Kentucky, gizzard shad and river herring make good bait. The smaller ones can be used on the hook whole, while the larger ones can be cut into chunks or strips. The guts from such fish are also good. Other fish such as small perch, sunfish, suckers, carp, small catfish, and bullheads are also taken.

Catfish have also been caught on fruits, berries, laundry soap, congealed chicken and animal blood, and various stink and doughball baits made from combinations of cheese, meat, fish, and flour.

When going catfishing it's a good idea to take along several different kinds of baits and try them all until you find which the fish want. Although catfish eat almost anything, they have their feeding periods and preferences when they want a certain kind of food and ignore all others.

Catfish have also been caught on slow-moving artificial lures such as plugs, jigs, spoons, and spinners. In a few spots they are deliberately fished for with the jigs or other artificials. In most waters, however, they are caught on lures being used for the more active game fish. The speedier channel catfish is more likely to be caught on artificial lures than the other species. But day in and day out, the natural baits are more dependable for all kinds of catfish.

The season for catfishing may begin as early as March or April in southern waters and run up to October or November. Farther north it

may start later and end earlier, but usually the months from May to October are best. They are more likely to be congregated in rivers below dams during May, June, and July when they are spawning. In the northern states catfishing is often good during the summer months. June is usually a good month in most areas.

The best time to go catfishing is when the river is rising from a recent rain and is becoming discolored. Then they start on a feeding binge and eat around the clock on foods washed by the rains into the river. After the water has been muddy for a few days the fishing may fall off since the catfish have filled their bellies. When the water is clear the best fishing takes place early in the morning, late afternoon and evening, and during the night. In fact, you can't choose a better time for catfishing than at night. That's when they leave their hideouts and roam the shallows and shoreline looking for food.

If you do fish during the daytime you have to locate the spots where catfish hide or lurk in the deeper water and holes. Then you should fish the underhanging banks, beneath rocks and ledges, stumps, logs, sunken trees, brush piles, tree roots, and similar spots. The deep pools, channels, and eddies are best during the daytime. At night you can try the rapids, riffles, and shallows near shore. Big catfish are often found in the deeper pools and channels below big dams. At Pickwick Dam in Tennessee, the best spots are "boils" which is the turbulent water flowing through the turbines and coming out of the openings.

This is mostly boat fishing and anglers in a small boat head close to the boils, lower their sinker and bait and drift slowly downstream. The outboard motor is running with the boat heading into the current as it backs slowly downriver. This is a dangerous method since you never know when water will be released from the turbines and one of the boils may erupt under the boat to capsize it.

Still other anglers like to head through the boils to the quieter water next to the dam and fish there. And still others run their boats up to the boils, then cut the motor and drift downstream bouncing bottom with their sinker and bait. Another method is to anchor your boat above a hot spot and then drift the bait into it.

This 100-pound catfish was caught in Tennessee. Most of the big catfish are found in southern waters. (TENNESSEE CONSERVATION DEPARTMENT)

From shore, fishermen cast out into the river with the sinker and bait and let it go down to the bottom. Then they put their rod in a forked branch or prop it against a log or rock and wait for a bite. A catfish is usually slow about taking a bait and must be given plenty of time. Don't try to set the hook on the first nibbles but wait until the fish really swallows the bait and starts moving off with it.

Anglers seeking channel catfish in the smaller, shallower rivers and creeks like to wade for the fish and drift the bait into likely looking spots. In the faster waters you can drift the bait without a float or bobber. But in the slower moving sections a bobber or float can be used to keep the bait moving with the current. The bait should be close to the bottom at all times. You can take a position in a rapid or riffle above a pool and let the bait wash down into the deeper water. Do this slowly with the bait held stationary for a few minutes in one spot, then lift the rod tip and let it move off downstream to a new area. You can also let the bait drift under overhanging trees or bushes, under log jams, tree roots, and overhanging banks.

In states where it is allowed catfish are caught on drop lines or hand lines with hooks and baits on the end, thrown out and tied to stakes, trees, or branches. Or trotlines may be stretched across a stream or river. These have short lines with hooks baited and tied to the main line at regular intervals. The trotlines are usually set in the evening and are allowed to remain in the water until morning when they are checked.

Another effective and popular way to catch catfish is by jugging. Years ago they used regular stone or glass jugs, but today two quart oil-cans are welded together or gallon cans are used. These are painted some light or gaudy color and a line with a hook is attached to the handle or ring on the float. This line will vary in length according to the depth of the river being fished. The bait must reach close to the bottom. Baits such as beef liver, beef heart, minnows, or other meats or fish baits are put on the hooks tied to the jugs or cans. Then they are put in a boat and when the fishing area is reached they are tossed overboard to form a group of floating cans. If the current is strong a strip of lead or sinker is added to the line above the hook. When a can starts to dance up and down or disappears and bobs up the anglers in the boat head for it and pull out the catfish. Jigging is usually most effective during the hot summer months when the river is low.

Still another method used legally or illegally, depending on which state you live in, is grabbling. Also called groping, tickling, and noodling it is a means of catching catfish with the bare hands. This is done mostly in late spring or during the summer months when catfish are holed up spawning and guarding their eggs. The grabbler probes with his arms in the holes under the banks or logs and a catfish attacks his hand. Then the braver individuals may shove their arms through the catfish's mouth and out through the gill opening. This provides a firm grip and the catfish can be hauled out. Other grabblers prefer to tickle the catfish along its belly slowly working their hands toward the gills. Then they quickly insert their fingers under the gill cover and grab the catfish to pull it out. But before you venture forth to do likewise check your state laws to see if grabbling is legal in your area.

A catfish, however, is at its best when caught on rod and reel. If you use the lightest tackle that is practical for the waters you are fishing and the size of the fish running you can have a lot of fun and sport. Channel catfish, especially, will put up a great scrap making fast runs and sometimes splashing around on the surface. But most catfish fight deep and bore toward the bottom for a submerged rock, log, tree root, or other spot where they can foul or cut your line. Big catfish will give you the most trouble and in some waters heavy tackle is the only answer to holding them and pulling them off the bottom.

Catfish are usually hooked deep and the smaller ones can be lifted into a boat or on shore if the line is strong enough. The larger ones can be netted with a wide-mouthed net or gaffed.

Catfish, of course, must be skinned before you eat them. This is done by cutting the skin around the head and down the back and belly. Pliers are used to grab the skin and it is pulled off toward the tail. Small catfish can be cooked whole but the larger ones can be filleted or steaked. They can be fried or stewed and catfish fries are popular in the Midwest and South.

Many rivers in the Midwest and South are noted for catfishing, such as the Mississippi, Missouri, Ohio, Tennessee, Illinois, White, and Green Rivers. The white catfish has been planted in the Great Lakes and in California where they are plentiful in the lower Sacramento and San Joaquin Rivers. White catfish are also found in the Connecticut River and many lakes and ponds in Connecticut. In Virginia they are found in the Potomac River. While in North Carolina they are common in the Cape Fear and Roanoke Rivers. White cat-fish reach a big size in South Carolina in the Santee-Cooper Reservoirs. Many rivers and reservoirs in Texas have catfish with the Rio Grande one of the best. In Florida the St. Johns River and its bulge, Lake George, are great catfishing waters. But there are many other waters in the states listed above and others are not listed which contain catfish. A little exploring and fishing with the right baits at the right time of year will determine whether catfish are present in specific rivers or lakes.

Chapter 23

BULLHEADS

The bullheads are smaller members of the catfish family, but what they lack in size they make up in numbers and popularity. This is the fish together with sunfish which is usually caught by small boys. But don't get the idea that bullheads are only for the youngsters and have nothing to offer older anglers. They are just as popular with many older anglers all over the country. In fact, it's a common sight to see several hundred men, women, and kids fishing for bullheads on levees, shores, and banks where these fish are numerous.

And bullheads are usually plentiful in most waters. Their ability to live in polluted or warm waters which chase away or kill other fish, makes them available to all even near large cities and towns. Actually, the bullhead is usually the prevalent species in many park ponds and lakes in big cities.

Three kinds of bullheads are found in the United States. One is the brown bullhead also called the speckled bullhead, pond catfish, red catfish, marble catfish, brown catfish, and pol-

lywog. It is an olive to brown color on the back and the sides are mottled with light and dark patches. The yellow bullhead is another species and is also called the pond bullhead. It has a white chin and whiskers, slightly rounded tail and a yellow belly. The third one is the black bullhead which is called the creek bullhead, black catfish and stinger. The body of this bullhead varies from greenish brown to black shading into a greenish bronze. It has a light vertical bar at the base of the tail.

Bullheads are also known as "horned pouts" in some areas. They are now found in many parts of the United States outside their original range. They are very popular as a pond fish on farms throughout the Midwest and South.

There is one drawback, however, in stocking them in farm ponds. Bullheads grow slowly but they breed rapidly and may overpopulate a pond or lake to the detriment of game fish such as trout or bass. If there are too many bullheads in a small body of water they may become stunted and fail to reach a good size. Because of

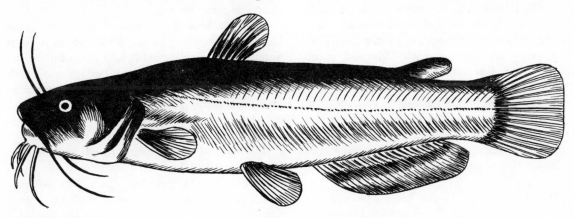

BULLHEAD

The bullhead is a bottom feeder like most members of the catfish family so keep your bait down on the mud, clay, sand, or rocks. (OHIO DEPARTMENT OF INDUSTRIAL AND ECONOMIC DEVELOPMENT)

this they should be caught as rapidly as possible or seined at regular intervals to reduce their numbers in farm ponds. In many states there are no closed seasons or bag limits on bullheads. You can fish for them the year round and take as many as you like.

It would be foolish to recommend any specific fishing tackle for bullheads because they can be caught on almost any outfit available. Cane poles are popular with kids and many older anglers. But you can also catch them on spinning rods and reels, bait-casting rods and reels, and fly rods. Of course, if you want to have the most sport and fun you should use the lightest tackle possible. There's a big difference in catching a bullhead on a big, heavy cane pole or hooking one on an ultralight spinning rod or fly rod.

Although bullheads have been known occasionally to follow and strike an artificial lure such as a plug, spoon, spinner, or fly, they are usually caught on natural baits. The list of such baits is long, but day in and day out the lowly earthworm takes the most bullheads. If you are using night crawlers one or two worms on a hook are sufficient. But when using the smaller garden worms or angleworms you can use a half-dozen or more on a hook.

Strips of beef liver or meat are often good baits. In fact, you can use pieces of meat from almost any animal or poultry to catch bullheads. Small minnows are excellent bait as are small pieces of almost any fish. Bullheads have also been caught on doughballs, bread, insects, and most of the baits used for catfish. (See the chapter on catfish for a list of these baits.)

Bullheads bite from spring to fall but the best fishing usually takes place starting about April in the South and during May, June, July, August, and September through most of their range. Although bullheads will bite during the daytime they are not too active in waters which are clear. The best fishing in rivers and creeks usually takes place when the water is rising from a recent rain or shower. When the water turns brown, the bullheads will bite all day long. In lakes you'll find your best fishing early in the morning, in the evening, and during the night. Cloudy or rainy days are better than clear, sunny days when fishing during the daytime. But as soon as it gets dark, bullheads become active and prowl the shallows and shorelines in search of food.

Many bullhead fishermen do most of their fishing at night and it can be a lot of fun. Take along a lantern or build a fire on shore, cast out your lines and wait for a bite. If bullheads are present in the waters being fished it won't be long before they find your baits and you get action.

Bullheads are gregarious by nature and where you find one there will usually be others. They like the slower pools and eddies in a stream or river. They prefer mud bottoms of rivers or lakes but are also found over gravel, sand, and rocky bottoms in many waters. Look for them under bridges, below dams and riffles, along undercut banks and tree roots.

In the quieter waters and in most lakes you can fish for bullheads with a cane pole or rod and reel without using a sinker. Usually the bait will go down to the bottom of its own accord. A float or bobber can be used to indicate bites. In faster waters such as rivers and streams or where you have to cast some distance a sinker can be used. This is usually attached to the end of your line and a few inches above it a short leader and hook is tied. Bullheads have large mouths so hooks in sizes No. 1 or 1/0 can be used. This rig is cast out and allowed to sink to the bottom. Then you can put your rod in a forked stick or prop it against something and wait for a bite. The click should be set on your rod especially when fishing at night. You can also use small dock bells to indicate bites at night when using two or three lines or rods.

When you get the first nibbles wait a few seconds more until the bullhead swallows the bait before setting the hook. A good-sized bullhead in a fast river will put up a good fight on light tackle but most fishermen using cane poles just yank them out of the water without much

ceremony, remove them from the hook and cast out for another one.

When you do catch a bullhead hold it carefully so that you don't get stuck with the sharp spines. These are toxic from a venom which is secreted at the base of the spine. But they aren't dangerous although the wound they leave may be painful and cause the fingers or hand to swell. The best way to remove a catfish is to grab the fish so that the spines emerge between your fingers and the fish can be held firmly. Still safer is to pin the fish to the ground with your foot and then remove the hook. Bullheads often clamp their jaws on a hook or swallow it deeply and a stick with a notch on one end or a hook disgorger is a big help. So is a pair of the long-nosed pliers sold to fishermen for holding fish and removing hooks.

Bullheads rarely come big with the average fish between ½ and 1 pound in weight. A few may reach as much as 3 or 4 pounds but such big specimens are rare in most waters.

Like most catfish, the bullhead makes good eating but must be skinned before eating. Most anglers cut the skin around the head, grab the edge with gripping pliers and pull it off the body. A quick way to do this without using pliers is to cut a slight depression just ahead of the dorsal fin on the fish's neck just deep enough to cut through the backbone. Then cutting away from your hand which grasps the head of the fish, remove the dorsal fin and spine. Then slit the skin on top of the bullhead's back all the way down to the tail. Finally you grab the fish's body near the tail with one hand and hold on to the head with the other hand and bend the two sections sharply causing the backbone to emerge. Grip the end of the backbone between your thumb and a knife blade and pull on the fish's head. This skins the fish and at the same time removes the entrails which stay attached to the head. It sounds complicated but once you get the knack it is easy and quick and a bullhead can be cleaned in a matter of seconds.

Bullheads are found in many parts of the United States with the brown bullhead ranging from Canada, throughout the Great Lakes, St. Lawrence region south to Virginia. A subspecies is found from southern Illinois to Arkansas, the Carolinas and Florida. The black bullhead is

Bullheads are most plentiful in the slower, lazy river and streams, and in lakes. (MISSISSIPPI A & I BOARD)

found from Canada to North Dakota, the Great Lakes region south to Colorado, Wyoming, Tennessee, and Kansas. A subspecies is found in Alabama, Texas, and Louisiana. The yellow bullhead is found from North Dakota through the Great Lakes to New York and south to Texas and the Tennessee River system. Another subspecies is found from New Jersey southward. Of course, as stated earlier, bullheads have also been stocked in many other areas, especially farm ponds.

Chapter 24

EELS

The first eel I ever caught as a young boy was taken in a small country brook where the current had pulled the worm and hook under the roots of a large tree. The bait rested there a few seconds, then I felt a sharp tug. I yanked on the pole and an eel about two feet long came flying out.

That was the end of fishing for that day. I grabbed my string of sunfish, and holding the squirming eel as far away from myself as possible, I ran almost all the way back to the farm which was a mile away. I thought that I had hauled in a snake!

This snakelike appearance of the eels has no doubt repelled many anglers who do their best to avoid catching them. But thousands of other anglers fish for eels often, because they have discovered that this unique fish can provide fun and is a table delicacy second to none.

The eel, of course, is a true fish like any fresh- or salt-water fish. It breathes in the water by means of gills like any other fish. A snake breathes out of the water by means of lungs. An eel has two small fins near the head and a long, continuous fin along the back and around the tail. A snake has no fins.

Eels vary in color from gray to greenish-brown to black on the back and this blends with a lighter white below on the belly.

For a long time the eel was a creature of mystery and little was known about its spawning or migrations. Ancient Europeans thought that eels originated spontaneously from slime, dew, grass, horsehair, and mud.

It was not until the middle 1800s that the first larva of an eel was examined by Dr. Karp, a German naturalist. But he thought it was a new species and failed to identify it as the larva of

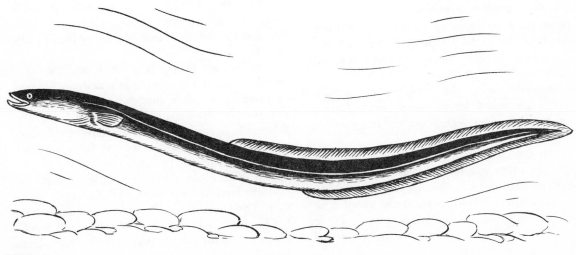

EEL

an eel. This was done in 1896 when two Italian ichthyologists identified it as the larva of the European common eel. Then in 1906 a Danish scientist named Johannes Schmidt began a series of investigations which lasted more than fifteen years and proved that both the American and European eels travel to the Sargasso Sea region near Bermuda to spawn.

The migrations of the common eel are even more remarkable than those of the salmon. Both the American eel and European eel spend most of their lives in fresh-water lakes, rivers, and streams. They look alike except that the American eel has from 103 to 111 vertebral segments, while the European eel has from 110 to 119. This has been challenged by a British scientist who claims there is only one eel—the American eel. However, his theory hasn't been accepted by many and for the present we'll assume that there are two species—the American eel and European eel.

Only the female eels are found in fresh water where they live anywhere from six to eight years before they mature. These "silver eels" descend the rivers in the autumn to meet the males which have been living in brackish and salt-water bays. Then they slowly move toward their spawning area in the region of the Sargasso Sea. Here in the deep water they lay their eggs and then die.

When the eggs hatch the larvae of the eels are tiny, less than a quarter of an inch long, shaped like a willow leaf and transparent. For a time the tiny eels remain several hundred feet below the surface of the ocean. Then they slowly rise to the warmer waters above.

Now the most amazing episode of all takes place. The American larvae start to drift and swim toward the west, while the European larvae move toward the east. Since the American larvae are closer they reach the coast in about a year. But the European larvae being much farther away from the continent, require three years to complete the journey.

When the larvae reach the coastlines of their respective continents they change from the leaf-like shape into the cylindrical form of the adult eel. They are still transparent, only about 2 or 3 inches long and are known as "glass eels" or "elvers." Soon they lose their transparency and take on the dark colors of their parents. Then

the females ascend the fresh-water rivers, while the males remain in the brackish and salt-water bays and estuaries.

The American eel is found along the East Coast from Labrador to the Gulf of Mexico. They migrate up the Mississippi River and its tributaries and are found in many states east of the Rocky Mountains.

To catch eels you can use ordinary hand lines, cane poles, spinning rods, spin-casting rods and bait-casting rods and fly rods. Most eels run pretty small, rarely more than a pound or two in weight so light tackle will provide the most fun.

Although an eel will strike a wet fly fished slow and deep at times, they are rarely interested in artificial lures. Natural baits are best for them and they feed mostly on or near the bottom poking their pointed snouts into every crevice or hole searching for food. They are more or less like the catfish in that they feed on a wide variety of animal matter. Eels will eat crayfish, frogs, worms, insects, and small fishes. Worms and small minnows usually make the best bait.

It is best to use a rather thick, heavy line and a long-shanked hook like the Carlisle in sizes No. 1 or 1/0. Eels will wrap themselves around in a line and will often swallow a hook deep. A long-shanked hook is easier to remove and is less likely to be swallowed all the way down. And a thick line is easier to untangle when an eel makes a mess out of it.

Eels can be caught from April to November in most waters but the spring and fall are the best times. If you can find a river where the eels are migrating to the sea in the autumn you'll have some great fishing in September and October. But the summer months also produce plenty of eels.

The best eel fishing is at dusk and throughout the night. They seem to bite actively for two or three hours after sundown, then there is a lull. Usually the darker the night, the better the fishing. Eels can also be taken during the daytime especially in rivers or creeks which are muddy from recent rains.

Eels will come into very shallow water at night to feed and are often found close to shore then. They hide during the daytime under ledges, banks, rocks, weeds, and roots. In small creeks and streams the deeper pools are the best places to fish.

Fishing for eels with rod and reel is a slow, waiting game with best results at dusk and at night. Worms, minnows, and pieces of meat or fish can be used for bait. (PHOTO BY JOHNNY NICKLAS, PENNSYLVANIA FISH COMMISSION)

Most eels are caught by still fishing from shore with the angler casting out his line and bait and letting it lie on the bottom. In lakes or quiet pools and eddies no sinker is needed, but in fast currents a small sinker is required. A weight is also good if you want to cast to a distant spot.

You can have more fun and catch more eels if you use more than one rod or line. Usually two, three, or more rods and lines are cast out and placed along the shore. You can set the click on your reels or attach the lines to small dock bells. This will warn you if you have a bite and is especially valuable at night when the line can't be seen. A lantern or light comes in handy at night for baiting the hooks and removing the eels.

When you catch an eel, haul it in quickly to prevent it from doubling up and tangling your line. A big eel caught in a rocky area can give you plenty of trouble by crawling into a hole, and unless your line is strong you'll probably break off and lose him. If caught over a muddy bottom or other area, free from obstructions you can fight a big eel on a light outfit for a few minutes. However, the long, slim body of an eel isn't built for fighting and the best he can do is tug, shake his body from side to side in an attempt to get free.

A potato sack to keep the eels in and a dry rag or a bucket of sand are necessary on any eel-fishing trip. When you bring an eel in, grab it with the rag or drop it into the sand and you'll be able to hold the eel firmly while removing the hook.

Another way to catch eels is by the old-time method of bobbing. To make an eel bob bait, take a long needle and attach several feet of fine linen thread. Now thread as many earthworms as are needed to fill the string and roll the whole mess into a ball. Wrap some more thread around the worms and then attach the whole works to a fishing line and a cane pole.

Lower this to the bottom of the lake or river at night and let it lie there. When you feel any bites and are sure that several eels are chewing on the worms start lifting the bait slowly toward the surface. Then when the eels are near the top of the water, lift them out quickly and swing them over a bushel basket or open potato sack. The eel's fine teeth get tangled in the thread

and they hang on for a short while, but soon start dropping off.

Eels can also be speared at night during the spring, summer, and fall months. This can be done from a boat with a light suspended at the bow or by wading in shallow water also with a headlight or searchlight. A wide spear with several barbed tines is best for this. Eels are also speared through the ice in rivers and salt-water bays when they hibernate in the mud.

Eels can also be taken in eel pots baited with dead fish, meat, or similar foods. They are caught in large numbers commercially in traps, racks, and seines in the autumn when they are migrating to the sea.

The female eels caught in fresh water usually run from about 1½ to 3 feet in length. Occasionally one over 3 feet and weighing several pounds is caught. A few eels do not mature sexually and may reach a length of 4 or 5 feet and weights up to 15 or 16 pounds. The males are much smaller running from 1 to 2 feet in length in the salt water and brackish bays where they live.

To skin an eel, first stun it by whacking its head against something solid. Then cut through the skin completely around the neck, but not into the meat. Now either hold the head with a dry rag or nail it down to a board. Grasp the loose flap of skin below the head with a pair of pliers and with a sharp pull toward the tail remove the skin.

Eels have a firm, sweet flesh and can be fried, pickled, or boiled. Smoked eels are considered a delicacy and bring a fancy price in the larger cities.

Anglers who pursue the wily trout or the fighting bass may turn up their noses when eels are mentioned, but the fact remains that many fishermen get a kick out of catching eels. In some sections of the country it is the only fishing which can be had in heavily polluted waters. The pollution has killed off or driven away the more delicate game fishes, but the eel doesn't seem to mind. He's tough, rugged and takes a long time to die, which is the only thing he's got in common with snakes besides the elongated shape. Year after year eels complete their fascinating life cycle and at the same time furnish food and sport for thousands of anglers.

Chapter 25

SHAD

There are records of shad being taken in the Connecticut River on rod and reel as early as 1869. Since then, many early anglers wrote of the excellent shad fishing they had usually when using flies and fly rods. But these anglers who enjoyed sport fishing for shad remained a handful until after World War II when spinning tackle came into use and more and more outdoor writers popularized fishing for shad. Now, thousands of anglers fish for shad not only along the Atlantic Coast but also along the Pacific Coast where shad were introduced from the East back in 1871.

Shad were so plentiful in the early days that they choked the rivers and were caught by the wagonload by the colonists and used for fertilizer. Atlantic salmon were also plentiful in those good old days and the colonists preferred salmon to the bony shad when it came to eating them. Later on the salmon started to disappear due to dams, pollution, and overfishing, and shad became popular. Then they too started to become less plentiful and by 1900 the runs of shad became small or nonexistent in many rivers. Then steps were taken to eliminate pollution and some of the dams were removed. Fishways were also established on dams which couldn't be destroyed. Gradually the shad have been making a comeback and fair runs have been re-established on some of the rivers.

The American shad is also called the common shad, white shad, Atlantic shad, jack and silver herring. Anglers have also dubbed it "white lightning" and "poor man's salmon" because of its fast, flashy, fighting qualities on the end of a line. The shad is a member of the herring family and is sometimes mistaken for the hickory shad —a close relative often found in the same waters.

The American shad has a deep, compressed body, greenish back with a metallic luster. The sides and belly are silvery and there are dark spots on the shoulder often followed by smaller spots.

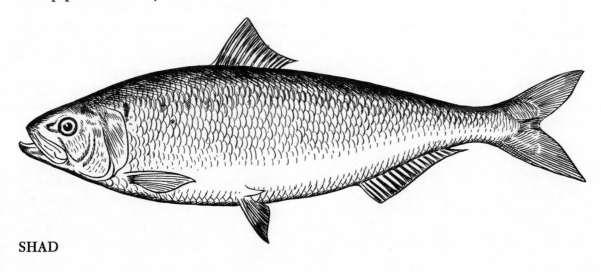

SHAD

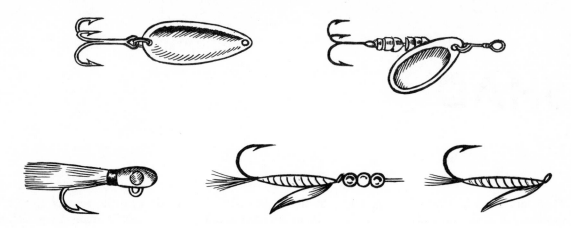

Lures used for shad

Shad are found along the Atlantic Coast from the St. Johns River in Florida to the St. Lawrence River in Canada. On the Pacific Coast they range from Southern California north to Alaska. Shad spend most of their lives in salt water but return to fresh-water rivers and streams to spawn. Although they eat little or no food during the fresh-water run they will hit lures and practically all shad are caught on rod and reel during the spawning journey.

You can use many different kinds of fresh-water outfits to catch shad. Bait-casting, spin-casting, spinning and fly rods have all been used. Shad lures are small and light and you should have a rod which can cast lures in the 1/16 to ½ ounce range. The most popular outfit is a light fresh-water spinning rod, and small spinning reel filled with 4- or 6-pound test line. This is best for casting from shore or a boat. For trolling, a similar outfit or slightly heavier spinning rod can be used. Fly rods which are used for trout or bass can also be used to cast flies for the silvery scrappers. These are best when casting from shore or shallow water or from boats. Light, limber bait-casting rods can also be used to cast lures from shore or boats and for trolling.

Shad flies which are usually simple lures are often effective when used with a fly rod or when let out in a strong current from a boat. These are usually tied on No. 3, 4, 6, or 8 hooks and consist of a body of silver tinsel and sparse,

white, red, or yellow feathers for wings. They are often used together with beads of various colors ahead of the hook. In fact, a hook wrapped with silver tinsel and two or three beads ahead of it will also catch shad. Other lures used for shad include small streamers and bucktails, unweighted for use with fly rods and weighted for use with spinning or casting rods. Small weighted spinners and small spoons will also take them. Tiny jigs can also be used and are especially effective for getting down in a swift current.

On the St. Johns River in Florida they often troll with a tandem rig having a small spoon attached by swivels to the line and another lure, usually a small yellow jig, attached to a 3-foot leader which in turn is attached to the swivel on the line. This is trolled and sometimes split-shot or clincher sinkers are added on the line to get the shad rig down into deeper water.

Shad are occasionally taken on natural baits such as worms, tiny minnows, and grass shrimp. But few anglers fish for them with baits and most prefer to use the flashy artificials which are usually effective.

The shad fishing season varies according to location, weather, and water temperature. It may start as early as December with good fishing during January, February, and March on the St. Johns River in Florida. Farther north it usually begins in April or May with May and June

This shad was caught in the St. Johns River in Florida where good fishing is often had during the winter months.
(FLORIDA STATE NEWS BUREAU)

Shad have a delicate mouth and must be fought with care. A wide-mouthed landing net is best for boating them.
(PHOTO BY JOHNNY NICKLAS, PENNSYLVANIA FISH COMMISSION)

the top months. In California it may start in March and continue through May. In Oregon and Washington, May and June are good months and the fishing may continue into July. It must also be remembered that on some of the longer rivers the shad takes more time to reach the upper reaches where fishing will be later than on the lower portions.

The time of day to go shad fishing will also depend on where you fish. On the St. Johns River shad rarely bite before 10 A.M. and usually quit around 4 P.M. Farther north good fishing is often had early in the morning and late afternoon and evening. In the Connecticut River it was found that shad like water temperatures around 67 or 68 degrees. They don't bite as well in northern rivers on raw, windy, cloudy days as they do on the bright, sunny ones. Sudden rains which raise the water and muddy the river may ruin the fishing until the water clears.

Above all, shad travel in schools and their behavior is highly unpredictable. There may be hours of inactivity—then suddenly they will start hitting. After having fast fishing for a few minutes or sometimes an hour or two, they may suddenly quit or leave. Then you can cast again for hours without getting a strike.

Since the shad are moving upstream to spawn they follow the main channels and strongest flow of water. You'll find them moving or darting in such currents. The best fishing is usually found in spots where there are obstructions such as falls, dams, shallow rapids which concentrate the shad in a small area. Often, you can see the shad lying in the current or the pools or swimming and milling around.

On some rivers it's easy to locate the best shad fishing spots since you'll find anglers lining the banks shoulder to shoulder casting toward the fish. The usual procedure is to cast the lure up and across the current and allow it to swing and sink toward the bottom. Most strikes will occur at the end of the arc when the lure starts to rise. Fly rod anglers may have to add a split-shot or two to the leader to get their lures down. The sinking fly lines are also a big help in getting the lure down to the fish. Usually the fly is allowed to drift naturally with little or no rod action. But lures can be jerked or twitched to make them flash.

Casting can also be done from an anchored or drifting boat, but most anglers prefer to troll. On the St. Johns River you troll with about 100 or 125 feet of line out and the lure travels a few feet down. Slow trolling up and down the river is practiced with the hot spots usually the bends or narrow stretches where the current speeds up.

On the West Coast they fish from an anchored boat—often two or three lines of boats will be tied up alongside each other. Then they drop the lures back in the current. In a strong current they use a rig with a three-way swivel. A 3-foot leader holding the lure is attached to one of the eyes on the swivel. A sinker is attached to another eye, usually about 2 or 3 feet below the swivel. And, of course, the fishing line is tied to the remaining eye on the swivel. The lure is generally a small spinner or spoon.

Shad will often hit a lure hard, but other times you'll feel only a series of light taps. Keep casting, however, since this shows that the fish are present and are interested in the lure.

When you hook a shad you'll know why it has been called white lightning. A shad will make a fast, long run, then leap out of the water so fast that your eyes can barely follow it. It is a game fish which will fight right up to the end and many are lost during the battle near the end. They have soft mouths and a sudden pull or shock will rip the hook out of their jaws. They must be played with extreme care and even then you'll probably lose more fish than you will land. A long-handled, wide-mouthed landing net is needed to scoop a shad up near the boat or in shallow water when wading.

Shad reach about 15 pounds in weight but most fish will average around 4 pounds. Nowadays a 7- or 8-pound shad is a big one. The females or "roe shad" grow larger than the males or "bucks." Shad roe is considered a delicacy and the females command a higher price in the fish market than the males. Shad are very bony and unless properly prepared are difficult to eat. Boning a shad to remove the fine bones is an art which few anglers know.

Starting in Florida we find shad in the St. Johns River in the northeastern part of the state. In Georgia and South Carolina the Savannah River has shad. The Edisto River in South Carolina also has some fishing for them. In North

Carolina they are found in the Cape Fear River. In Virginia they move up the James and Potomac Rivers. In Maryland they are found in the Potomac, Susquehanna River, and other streams and rivers entering Chesapeake Bay. In New Jersey, Pennsylvania, and New York they are found in the Delaware River. There are also runs up the Hudson River in New York. Probably the top fishing spot for shad is the Connecticut River in Connecticut. Here such spots as the Enfield Dam, Windsor Locks Bridge, and Holyoke are famous for their shad fishing. The Farmington River and its tributaries in Connecticut also have some shad fishing.

On the West Coast shad are found in California in the American River, Russian River, Sacramento River, and Feather River. In Oregon, the Columbia River, Coos Bay, Coos River, Sandy River, Willamette River, and Umpqua River have shad runs.

On the West Coast many anglers who formerly were strictly salmon and steelhead fishermen have tried shad fishing and have become enthusiasts. A few even claim that pound for pound the shad will outfight a steelhead or salmon.

This successful angler is holding a string of shad taken in the Delaware River, near Milford, Pennsylvania. (PHOTO BY JOHNNY NICKLAS, PENNSYLVANIA FISH COMMISSION)

Chapter 26

CARP

No fresh-water fishing guide would be complete unless the carp was included among its pages. Although many anglers, especially the specialists and purists, may disagree, the carp is highly popular with many thousands of fresh-water anglers in this country.

However, the carp still hasn't attained the same popularity in this country that it has in Europe. There, carp fishing is a time-honored sport and carp fishermen are a highly skilled group who take their sport seriously. They prepare their tackle and baits with utmost care, check the weather, select their spots, walk carefully, and fish for many hours. If they catch a good-sized carp they consider it a worthwhile trophy and real big ones have even been mounted.

At one time there were no carp in the United States, or in Europe for that matter. Carp were originally found in Asia and were especially plentiful in China where they have been raised in ponds for over 2500 years. From China they were introduced to Europe around the thirteenth century. They were present in England during Izaak Walton's time for he wrote about carp in his classic *The Compleat Angler*.

In many European countries carp were raised in ponds for food and were considered a delicacy. Even to this day tons of carp are cultivated selectively in ponds for sale to fish markets.

The very first introduction of carp into the United States is hard to pin down, but there are records of carp being brought over from Holland as early as 1832 by a Captain Henry M. Robinson. He kept them in a pond near Newburgh, New York, and it is said that some of the carp escaped into the Hudson River. A Californian, J. A. Poppe, introduced carp into that state in 1872. The fish were brought over from Holstein, Germany, and placed in a private pond in

CARP

When carp become too plentiful they are often thinned out by seining or poisoning a lake with chemicals. (NORTH DAKOTA GAME & FISH DEPARTMENT)

Sonoma County. Of eighty-three carp only five survived the trip but these spawned and soon were numerous enough to be sold and stocked in many waters in the West.

But the real march of the carp began in 1877 when the United States Fish Commission imported 345 carp from Germany and placed them in ponds in Druid Hill Park in Baltimore, Maryland. From there they were transferred to Babcock Lake in Washington, D.C. By 1879 the lake produced 12,265 carp. Soon there were shipments of young carp going out to twenty-five states and territories. By 1880 there were two thousand applications for carp.

Then, by 1900, carp had become so plentiful that many fresh-water anglers turned against them. At that time, also, other game fish started to get scarce and many anglers blamed the carp for this decrease. They accused the carp of eating fish and spawn, muddying the waters, lacking in food value and not being much as a game fish.

We now know that carp can make waters unsuitable for game fish with their rooting, feeding, and spawning habits. They compete for living space and food with the game fish. They roil the waters and make them unsuitable for spawning for such fish as black bass and sunfish.

But it has also been found that carp do not eat the spawn of other fish. And the carp has been blamed unfairly for conditions which are the result of siltation, pollution, fluctuating water levels, and warm water temperatures. There are many such waters in which game fish cannot live or reproduce. But the hardy carp often thrives and multiplies in such waters and takes over. Thus the carp provides fishing in many ponds, rivers, and lakes unsuitable for other fish.

So while many anglers and some fish and game departments regard the carp as a pest in certain waters, in other waters and among many fresh-water anglers the carp is a highly regarded sport fish. The carp is here to stay and can provide a lot of fun and sport as many anglers have discovered.

Although there is only one species of carp in the United States they have been divided into three types: "scaled carp" are those which are completely covered with scales; those that have patches or large irregular scales are called "mir-

ror carp"; and those that have no scales are called "leather carp." Of the three, the completely scaled variety is the most common. Carp are also called German carp, golden carp, silver carp, mud carp, mudhog, waterhog, riverhog, and bugle-mouthed bass.

The carp resembles its relative—the goldfish and the fish known as the buffalo which is native to this country. The carp is usually olive-green on the back with bronze sides and white or yellow belly. It has a long dorsal fin with a serrated spine in front. The carp's sucker-type mouth is toothless but it does have teeth in its throat. It has two barbels or "whiskers" on each side of the mouth.

Carp fishermen use all kinds of tackle from an ordinary hand line or drop line to salt-water rods and fly rods. In waters where the fish aren't too big a light spinning rod can be used. But for all-around carp fishing in waters where big fish are present a heavier spinning rod and reel is preferred. This can be a one or two-handed heavy fresh-water spinning rod or light salt-water type. The reel can be a large fresh-water model or light salt-water kind. It should hold at least 150 to 200 yards of 8- or 10-pound test line. Another good outfit for carp fishing is a bait-casting rod and reel filled with 14- or 18-pound test line.

There are places and times where carp can be caught on artificial lures such as bass bugs and flies. This is especially true during the summer months when carp may be feeding on insects such as Japanese beetles. Then you use a fly rod and cast to the fish with a bass bug, wet fly, or streamer and sometimes they'll take it. Carp have also been caught occasionally on plugs, spoons, spinners, and jigs. But you can't depend on them to take such lures very often so most carp fishermen resort to natural baits.

At the top of the list as a carp bait is the time-honored doughball bait. These are usually prepared from flour or corn meal and various sweetening or flavoring mixtures are added. You can make such a bait quickly and easily by taking a cup and a half of boiling water and adding a cup and a half of corn meal to it. This should be stirred over a low flame for about five or six minutes. You can add about two or three tablespoons of sugar or molasses to the corn meal.

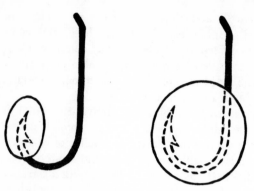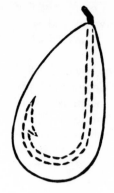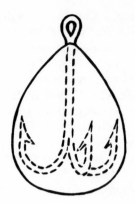

Doughball baits on hooks for carp

When the corn meal becomes thick and sticks to the sides of the pot it is ready. When it cools it is taken out and kneaded until it is thick. You can keep the bait in a refrigerator until it is used. Wrap it in aluminum foil or wax paper to keep it from drying out.

Doughball bait is used either on a single hook or a small treble hook. Single hooks such as the Eagle Claw types in sizes No. 1 or 2 for small fish and No. 2/0 to 5/0 for big fish can be used. These hooks can be covered entirely right up to the eye forming a large, pear-shaped bait. This will also provide weight for casting and sinkers need not be used in quiet lakes. But sometimes the carp prefer smaller baits and then you make a small doughball which just covers the bend of the hook or an even smaller one which covers only the point and barb.

When using a treble hook you can cover the entire hook right up to the eye. The bait stays on better and longer on a treble hook but this hook gets fouled more quickly on rocky or weedy bottoms.

Another good bait for carp is a loaf of fresh white bread. Just break off a chunk from the inside, knead it to form a ball and put it on the hook.

Carp have also been caught on many other baits such as fresh and cooked corn kernels, fresh and canned peas and lima beans, parboiled potatoes and parsnips, mulberries, marshmallows, hominy, meat, minnows, fresh-water clams and mussels, soft-shelled crayfish, and worms.

No expert carp fisherman in Europe would go carp fishing without first baiting the waters to attract carp to the area. This is similar to chumming in salt-water where you scatter some kind of fish food to attract fish to the boat or shore. In carp fishing you can scatter boiled potatoes, oatmeal, bread, canned corn, etc., all around in the area for two or three days before you start to fish. This should bring the carp around and you don't have to wait so long for a bite. However, baiting or chumming is illegal in many states or waters so check your local laws before doing this.

The best carp fishing usually takes place in the spring of the year during May and June when carp start to feed after a long winter fast. At this time they are also spawning and come into shallow water near shore. In the spring they can often be caught throughout the day. Later on during the hot summer months they move into deeper water and do not bite very well during the middle of the day. At such times the best fishing is usually had early in the morning, in the evening, and at night. Another peak fishing period often takes place in the fall of the year during September and October when they feed actively again a good part of the day.

Carp can adapt themselves to many different kinds of waters but they prefer lakes, ponds, rivers, and streams having mud bottoms and a lot of vegetation. They are most numerous in such waters and less abundant in the rocky rivers or lakes with hard bottoms. They also like the warmer, quieter and slow-moving rivers or

A carp about ready to give up. The big ones have a lot of power and endurance and put up a long fight. (PHOTO BY JOHNNY NICKLAS, PENNSYLVANIA FISH COMMISSION)

streams rather than the colder, fast-moving waters. They often gather below dams and the quiet pools and coves, shallow bays, lagoons, and swampy or marshy areas.

You can also see carp swimming near shore or lying near the surface in schools of varying numbers. Other times you can see or hear them leaping out of the water. In the spring when they come very close to shore to spawn you can see and hear them splashing loudly in the water right next to dry land.

The carp is a smart, wary, and cautious fish and the quiet approach is best. Keep out of sight or crouch low so that the carp won't see you or your shadow. Walk softly and don't make any unnecessary noises of stamping and running on shore.

Carp do not rush a bait like a bass or trout, but feed very slowly and deliberately mostly along the bottom grubbing in the mud and vegetation for their food. They may pick up a bait and drop it several times before they finally take it for good. Most carp fishermen use two or three rods which they place in forked sticks along the bank. They cast out, let the bait sink to the bottom, then set the clicks on their reels.

The first indication of a bite will be a slight movement of the line where it enters the water. Don't try to set the hook when you see the first nibbles. Keep waiting and if the carp decides to take the bait, the line will suddenly straighten out and rise from the water. That's the time to grab the rod and set the hook.

If you are using light tackle you'll probably be surprised at the speed and strength of a carp. The small ones are fast and are often mistaken for bass or other game fish when they make their runs. A big carp will be slower but will often take off like a jet plane and packs plenty of power in its run. They also have plenty of endurance and you can't rush or horse them when using light tackle. The best procedure is to play the carp until it is exhausted when it can be beached, netted, or gaffed.

The carp is not protected in most waters and fishing for them is allowed by various methods in many states most of the year. They are shot with bow and arrow when they come into shallow water near shore to spawn or feed. They are also speared with a long-handled spear mostly at night from a boat using a powerful light. Carp are also snatched or snagged with single or treble hooks on the end of a strong line and pole when they run up narrow streams or canals or whenever they congregate in any numbers. In the winter they are snagged through the ice in areas where they are hibernating on the bottom. And in recent years skin-divers have taken many carp with spear guns in waters where such underwater hunting is allowed.

Most of the carp you catch on rod and reel will weigh from 2 to 10 pounds. But many carp from 10 to 30 pounds are caught in waters where they reach this size. Carp in the 40- and 50-pound class are sometimes taken by commercial fishermen. The largest caught on rod and reel weighed 55 pounds 5 ounces, and was caught in Clearwater Lake, Minnesota, on July 10, 1952, by Frank J. Ledwein. Carp are believed to reach 80 or 90 pounds in weight.

What do you do with carp after you catch them? Eat them, of course, because if properly prepared they make a fine meal. In Europe and some of the larger cities in the United States carp are sold alive and dead and are relished by gourmets. Any good fish cookbook will have recipes on preparing and cooking carp.

When carp come into shallow water to feed or spawn they can be shot by archers. This requires quiet stalking and is most successful when the water is slightly muddy. (TENNESSEE GAME AND FISH COMMISSION)

Chapter 27

SUCKERS

Suckers, like sunfish, are very popular with the younger anglers throughout the country. But a surprising number of older anglers also fish for suckers early in the spring. When word gets around that the suckers are running in a nearby stream there's a rush of men, women, and children to those waters. In a short time there's standing room only as the eager anglers line up to catch these fish. Suckers are usually the first fish to run in any numbers early in the spring soon after the ice is out. Many anglers who can't wait to start fishing welcome these rubber-lipped fish after the long winter months. Sucker fishing is a relaxing type of fishing—you bring a chair, build a fire or light a stove, make coffee, and then sit back and wait for a bite.

Since there are almost one hundred different kinds of suckers found in North America there is usually some brook, river, or lake nearby in every state which contains these fish. However, only a few kinds are big enough to warrant being included as sport fish and which bite readily on a hook. One of these is the white sucker also called the common sucker, black sucker, and rainbow sucker. Another is the redhorse sucker also known as the redfin and redfin sucker. Still another is the longnosed sucker or northern sucker. These are the three main species of suckers caught by anglers but there are many others to be found in various areas which are taken at times. The white sucker has a wide range from Canada southward to New Mexico, Arkansas, Oklahoma, and Georgia. The northern redhorse suckers are found from eastern Canada to the Great Lakes—St. Lawrence watershed south to New York and west to Montana, Arkansas, and Kansas. The longnosed sucker is found from the St. Lawrence River and the Great Lakes westward to the upper Missouri basin and to the upper Columbia and north to Alaska. Still other species of suckers are found in our southern and western waters.

Suckers vary in color depending on the species but they are all similar in their general outline and mouth structure. They have suckerlike, fleshy lips, underslung mouths, large scales, and large soft-ray fins.

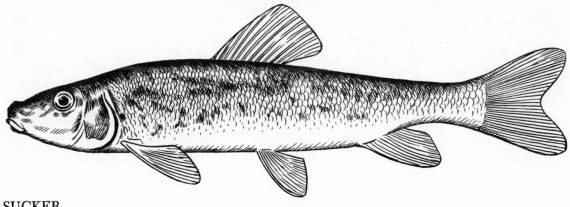

SUCKER

*Suckers are most readily caught early in the spring soon after the ice is out. This string was taken in the Lehigh River, Pennsylvania. (*PHOTO BY JOHNNY NICKLAS, PENNSYLVANIA FISH COMMISSION*)*

Suckers are caught on all kinds of fishing tackle from ordinary hand lines or drop lines to fancy casting outfits. Probably the cane or glass poles catch more suckers in the smaller brooks and streams than any other outfit. A fly rod provides a lot of sport on these narrow, confined waters. On the larger, wider rivers and lakes a light bait-casting or light spinning outfit is used.

Every once in a while you'll hear of a sucker grabbing a wet fly, nymph, or streamers being fished by a trout angler. Or they may grab a lure fished for bass or panfish. But this doesn't happen often enough to make it worthwhile to fish for suckers with such lures.

Most suckers are taken on natural baits such as worms which are the top bait early in the spring. The smaller earthworms are much better than the larger night crawlers. Usually one worm will catch them but other times two or three small worms on a hook are better. Another good bait later on during the summer months is the tail of a crayfish peeled down to the white meat and wrapped around a hook. Still another effective bait is the soft insides from a fresh-water clam or mussel. Cut this meat into small squares and use it on a small hook. Still other baits for suckers include grubs, insects, small pieces of meat, and doughballs. All of these should be used on a small hook ranging from No. 2 to No. 8 in size depending on the size of the suckers being sought.

The best time of the year to catch suckers is early in the spring as soon as possible after ice-out when the warm rains swell the streams. Then the suckers move up the narrow creeks, streams, and brooks to spawn. This may occur as early as February and March along their southern range and as late as May or June farther north. April is usually a good month in many areas.

Later on during the summer months suckers are harder to catch because they scatter more widely and do less feeding during the hot weather. You'll often see them then in small schools suspended midway between the surface and the bottom. At such times they aren't interested in baits and are hard to hook. However, if you see them feeding along the bottom you can sometimes make them take a bait by casting it in front of them and letting it lie quietly until they approach it.

That's one way to locate suckers when the water is clear—by watching until you spot them lying, swimming, or feeding below the surface. In the early spring you can look for concentrations of fishermen along the banks. Then they may be in the riffles or just below them spawning or getting ready to spawn. But they also gather in pools just below riffles and dams. Suckers will bite all day long in the spring, even when the water is too high and too muddy from recent rains. Of course, if the water is too high or too muddy it may stop the fishing. But as soon as it drops and starts to clear you can try fishing again.

Still fishing is done by casting out your baited hook with a cane pole or casting rod or spinning rod and letting it lie on the bottom quietly. If you are fishing in a strong current or want to cast out a good distance in a lake or big river you can add a small sliding sinker above the hook. Or you can tie the sinker on the end of the line and then tie a leader and hook a few inches above it. The main thing to remember is that the baited hook should lie on the bottom without moving. And it's a good idea to cover the point and barb of the hook with the bait.

Suckers feed slowly but deliberately somewhat like carp moving along the bottom and sample different kinds of tiny animal and vegetable matter. They'll come across your bait sooner or later when feeding but they are rarely in a hurry to take it quickly. So plenty of time must be given to allow them to mouth the bait. Don't strike at the first light nibbles—wait until the line starts to move away fast before you set the hook.

Most suckers put up a disappointing fight and rarely show any speed or endurance. But every so often a big specimen in fast water hooked on light tackle will take off and protest being hauled in. Such battlers have often been mistaken for trout, bass, or other game fish.

Another way to catch suckers, which may not be exactly sporting, is by snagging or snatching. This is done mostly in the spring when they are concentrated in thick schools. Here you drag a series of treble hooks on a line with a sinker on the end for weight through the fish hoping to foul-hook one through the body.

Still another way is by gigging or spearing with a long-handled spear. This, too, is done in

Suckers can be shot with bow and arrow as well as speared or snagged. This archer is all set to let go in the Au Sable River, Michigan. (FRED BEAR ARCHERY PHOTO)

shallow water when the suckers are moving up to spawn. It can be done in the daytime but is usually most successful at night. You can do it on the larger rivers and lakes along shore in a boat with a light in the bow. Or you can wade in the shallow water near shore or in the rapids of streams using a headlight and searchlight to spot the fish.

However, before doing any snagging or gigging, check your local fish and game laws to make sure the method is legal in your state or the waters being fished.

Suckers usually average anywhere from 10 to 16 inches in length and weigh up to a pound or so. But white suckers have been known to reach 30 inches in length and a weight of 8 pounds.

The redhorse sucker also reaches a large size up to 2 feet in length and a weight of 8 or 10 pounds.

Suckers are good food fishes but they have never become popular with anglers because of their small bones. Even so, large numbers are caught commercially and sold in the larger cities. They have sweet, tasty flesh which is at its best early in the spring when it is firm. They aren't too good during the summer months when they turn soft and may also have a muddy flavor from certain waters. The bones can be removed from the larger fish and they can be cut crosswise in the smaller ones. Then frying in deep fat or oil will usually soften the bones. Suckers can also be baked and boiled.

Chapter 28

OTHER FISHES

There are several other fishes which are taken on rod and reel in fresh water which deserve attention. Some are not too numerous or have too limited a range to become popular. Others are not available to any number of anglers and still others do not bite too readily or are difficult to catch. And still others may require special knowledge or techniques and methods not known to most anglers.

One group of fishes neglected or overlooked by many anglers are the whitefish. These silvery fish with large, smooth scales and forked tails are fairly numerous and are being discovered as a sport fish by more and more anglers. Although there are many species of whitefish found in North America only three are highly valued as sport fish at the present time.

One of the largest and most numerous is the lake whitefish which ranges from New York to New England, Canada, Newfoundland, Labrador, and Alaska. It is very common in the Great Lakes region where millions are caught commercially.

The cisco or lake herring is another species which resembles the lake whitefish and has many of the same habits. It is found in many lakes and some rivers in the Great Lakes region and in Canada and Alaska.

The other member of this group is the mountain whitefish also called the Rocky Mountain whitefish. It is found mostly in lakes and streams in the West from the Rocky Mountains westward to the Pacific and British Columbia. It is most plentiful in Montana, Wyoming, Utah, Idaho, Oregon, and Washington.

Most of the tackle used for other game fish can be utilized for whitefish. For deep fishing the spinning rod and bait-casting rod can be used. For shallow water and surface fishing the fly rod is good. The lighter, limber rods are best because whitefish don't run too big and have tender mouths.

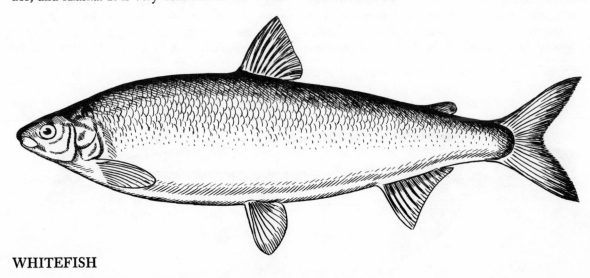

WHITEFISH

Whitefish will often hit wet flies, dry flies, tiny streamers or bucktails, jigs, spoons, and spinners. They'll also take natural baits such as small, live minnows, dead minnows, cubes of fish meat, salmon eggs, and insects.

It's a common practice when fishing for whitefish to "chum" the area ahead of time for several days. Then the whitefish tend to gather in that spot where they get a free handout. You can use canned sweet corn, boiled rice, tiny pieces of fish or meat for chum.

You'll find lake whitefish at various depths depending on the seasons and time of year. In spring and fall they may be in depths from 10 to 60 feet deep, while in the summer they may be up to depths of 100 feet or more. Lake whitefish tend to gather around shoals or river mouths. During the summer they may come up to the surface to feed on insects and then you can see them dimple the surface. During the winter they can be caught through the ice in water from 20 to 50 feet deep.

When lake whitefish or ciscoes are rising for flies you can often catch them on dry flies. Rocky Mountain whitefish will also hit wet flies in the streams where they are found. The fishing for them is usually best in the winter along riffles which are not covered by ice.

Casting and trolling with tiny spinners and spoons very slowly will often take lake whitefish and ciscoes.

Bait fishing is done near the bottom in spring, summer, fall, and winter for lake whitefish and ciscoes. Small, No. 6, 8, or 10 hooks baited with tiny live or dead minnows or cubes cut from larger fish can be used with or without a sinker depending on depth. A hooked whitefish often puts up a surprising fight somewhat like a trout. It may thrash on the surface, roll, twist, then bore deep. Those found in streams like the Rocky Mountain species are exceptionally lively and strong. Any whitefish must be handled carefully on the end of the line because they have a tender mouth and a hook pulls out easily.

Most lake whitefish caught will range from 1 to 5 pounds in weight and they have been caught commercially up to 15 or 20 pounds in the past. Ciscoes average from ½ to 1 pound in weight and have been known to reach 8 pounds. Rocky Mountain whitefish average about a pound and sometimes reach 3 or 4 pounds.

Whitefish are highly prized and have a sweet, delicious flesh which can be fried or baked. Smoked whitefish is a delicacy which is sold in many of our larger cities.

The sturgeon is another fish which is not often caught by anglers on rod and reel but which offers the nearest thing to big-game fishing in inland waters. There are several species of sturgeon found in North American waters but the one usually caught by anglers is the white sturgeon. This is the largest of the sturgeons in our waters, sometimes reaching 12 feet and weighing over a thousand pounds. The white sturgeon is found in rivers from California to Alaska. They run up these rivers to spawn and go far inland. One of the best spots to catch them is in Snake River, Idaho. Anglers, fishing for striped bass, salmon, and steelhead in Pacific Coast rivers, often hook them by accident but only the smaller ones are landed on the light tackle used.

If you want to catch sturgeon you have to equip yourself with heavy tackle. Although fish

STURGEON

This sturgeon was speared through the ice in Lake Winnebago, Wisconsin. (WISCONSIN CONSERVATION DEPARTMENT)

up to 360 pounds have been taken on heavy salt-water spinning tackle, a conventional surf rod and reel or salt-water big-game rod and reel is much better. Large hooks from 8/o to 12/o are used on a short leader tied above a sinker. In heavy rivers such as the Columbia and Willamette in Oregon and Washington up to 20 ounces of sinker may be needed to anchor the bait on the bottom in the strong current. Lines testing from 50 to 80 pounds are often used on the salt-water reels. Such baits as sardines, smelts, and lamprey eels are used for bait.

Sturgeon are usually found in the deeper pools of fairly fast-flowing water along the main current. A hooked sturgeon is not a spectacular fighter but is powerful and has plenty of endurance. The fight may last an hour or two or longer depending on the size of the fish and strength of the current. Most of those over 300 or 400 pounds are eventually lost.

Sturgeon on the Pacific Coast are caught all year round but the spring, early summer, and winter months are usually most productive.

The lake sturgeon or rock sturgeon is another one which is sometimes caught on rod and reel. They are also speared through the ice in Wisconsin lakes.

The sturgeon, as almost everyone knows, is an expensive fish which is the source of genuine caviar. But the meat can also be eaten fresh when fried, broiled, or baked. Smoked sturgeon is sold in stores in many of the larger cities especially in the East.

Another fish which is not too well known to many anglers but which can provide some sport at times is the fresh-water drum. Also known as the drum, sheepshead, gray bass, silver bass, white perch, grunt, grunter, croaker, grinder, gou, and gaspergou. It is a member of the drum family which includes many species of drums and croakers in salt water. Most of these fish and the fresh-water drum are capable of making a "croaking" or "drumming" sound hence the name "drum."

The fresh-water drum is found from the Hudson Bay drainage south to Lake Champlain and in the Great Lakes drainage through the Mississippi River region south to the Gulf of Mexico.

It lives in lakes, rivers, and streams in clear or muddy waters and usually prefers shallow waters near shore. It can be caught on almost any fresh-water tackle such as that used for bass. Most of the fresh-water drum hooked on artificial lures are caught when anglers are casting for other fish.

To catch them deliberately a natural bait such as a soft-shelled crayfish, shrimp, worm, or piece of fish is best. This should be fished on the bottom since the drum feeds on clams, mussels, snails, and crayfish.

Fresh-water drum average from 2 to 5 pounds with occasional 15- or 20-pounders being taken. There are records of this fish reaching 50 to 60 pounds. It is not considered as a particularly good food fish but is eaten quite a bit in the South.

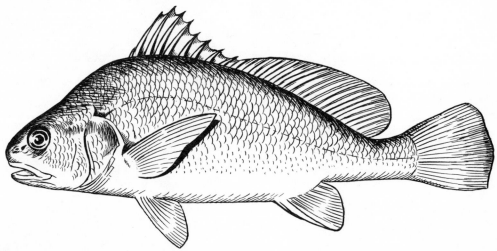

SHEEPSHEAD (fresh-water drum)

Smelt are caught with dip nets at night when they enter streams to spawn. (PHOTO BY JOHNNY NICKLAS, PENNSYLVANIA FISH COMMISSION)

A more popular fish is the American smelt also known as the salt-water smelt, fresh-water smelt, frostfish, and icefish. This is a slender, silvery fish with a translucent green back. It is found from Labrador south to New York, in Newfoundland, New Brunswick, Nova Scotia, Ontario, Quebec, the Great Lakes region, and many rivers and lakes in New England.

Smelt run up into fresh water from brackish or salt-water bays and estuaries to spawn in the spring soon after the ice is out. In the larger lakes they also enter rivers or streams emptying into the lake. This may take place in March, April, or May depending on water temperatures.

During these spawning runs, millions of smelt are caught with dip nets or scoop nets at night. The congregation of men, women, and kids all engaged in smelt-dipping on some of the rivers emptying into the Great Lakes is a sight to see. You need hip boots or waders, a flashlight or headlight and a long-handled dip net. Then you wade in shallow water and draw the wide-mouthed net to scoop up the silvery fish.

Smelt are also caught on tiny hooks baited with small minnows, pieces of fish, small shrimp, or bits of worm. The best fishing is usually during the fall, winter, and spring months in brackish or salt waters. Occasionally they'll also hit a fly or a tiny, bright lure. And on the larger lakes like New York's Lake Champlain they can be caught through the ice during the winter months. Then they will take a small minnow or slice of fish fished near the bottom. The bait should be raised and lowered at regular intervals to attract the smelt.

Most of the smelt caught will range from 6 to 8 inches and they reach about 12 inches. Fried smelt make delicious eating and annually tons are caught commercially and served in restaurants or sold in fish markets.

A fish sometimes caught by anglers is the buffalo fish. There are three species: the big-mouthed buffalo fish, black buffalo fish, and the smallmouthed buffalo fish. They belong to the sucker family and resemble the carp. They also have many of the same habits as the carp since they prefer sluggish waters and feed on many of the same foods. Buffalo fish are not too common in our northern states but are found mostly in the Mississippi River region. However, some are found as far north as Minnesota in the lakes and rivers.

But most of the buffalo fish that are caught on rod and reel are taken in southern waters on doughballs for bait. They come big, at times, with fish reaching 4 feet and 60 pounds having been reported. Those that are taken from clean waters are well flavored and make good eating. But those caught from muddy, weedy waters may have a muddy flavor.

Not many anglers realize that the minnow family can provide great sport on rod and reel. Of course, the carp which belongs to this family is well known and popular with many anglers. (See the chapter in this book devoted to this fish.) But there are other members of the minnow family which can be caught on rod and reel. One of the largest is the squawfish of which there are several species. They reach up to two feet in length and a weight of several pounds.

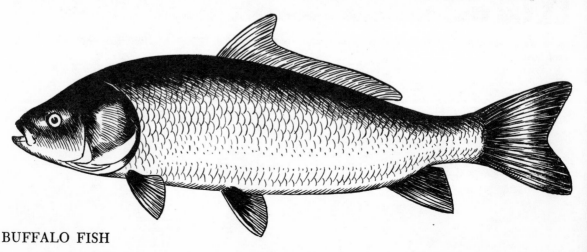

BUFFALO FISH

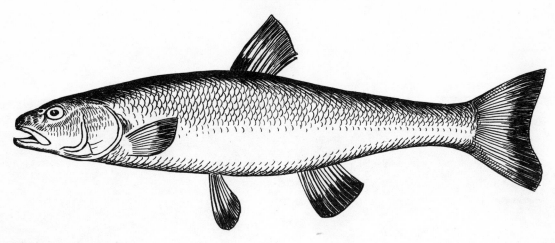

CHUB OR FALLFISH

They'll grab a lure or bait and put up a spirited fight in fast water. The squawfishes are found mostly in our Western states.

Another member of the minnow family which can provide good sport is the fallfish. It is found from Canada south to Virginia along the East Coast. It has been called the Mohawk chub, Delaware chub, white chub, silver chub, and just plain chub.

Many fallfish are taken by trout or bass fishermen using flies, lures, or natural baits. They will hit dry and wet flies, nymphs, streamers, spoons, spinners, and tiny plugs. In natural baits they'll take worms, minnows, crayfish, hellgrammites, and various insects.

Fallfish are often found in the larger rivers and streams in many of the same spots inhabited by trout or bass. They are caught either by casting and some are hooked while trolling. When first hooked they put up a fast, lively fight and have been often mistaken for a trout or small bass. But they lack the endurance of these fish and after the first few short runs and thrashing around they soon give up.

Fallfish or chubs run from 6 to 10 inches with a few reaching 18 or 20 inches. When caught, they should be cleaned as soon as possible and kept on ice or else they'll turn soft and unfit for the table. Those taken from cold, clean waters make the best eating. Their flesh is sweet and delicious although there are some fine bones present which must be removed.

A good-sized fallfish like this one can put up a satisfactory fight on light tackle. (PHOTO BY JOHNNY NICKLAS, PENNSYLVANIA FISH COMMISSION)